LEADERSHIP
AND LEARNING

LEADERSHIP AND LEARNING

Personal Change in a Professional Setting

Barry C. Jentz and Joan W. Wofford

McGRAW-HILL BOOK COMPANY

New York   St. Louis   San Francisco
Auckland   Bogotá   Düsseldorf   Johannesburg   London   Madrid
Mexico   Montreal   New Delhi   Panama   Paris   São Paulo
Singapore   Sydney   Tokyo   Toronto

Thomas Quinn and Michael Hennelly were the editors for this book. Christopher Simon was the designer. Thomas G. Kowalczyk supervised the production. It was set in Electra with display lines in Avant Garde by Black Dot, Inc.

Printed and bound by R. R. Donnelley and Sons.

Library of Congress Cataloging in Publication Data

Jentz, Barry C.
  Leadership and learning.

  Includes index.
  1. School superintendents and principals—Case studies. 2. Leadership—Case studies. 3. School management and organization—Case studies.
  I. Wofford, Joan, joint author. II. Title.
  LB2831.9.J46   371.2   79–9930
  ISBN 0–07–032497–2

1 2 3 4 5 6 7 8 9 RRD RRD 7 9 8 0 3 2 1 0 9

This book is dedicated to

KIYO MORIMOTO

*Associate Director
Bureau of Study Counsel
Harvard University*

and

*Idaho potato farmer,
frustrated opera singer,
certified army cook.*

Contents

Preface   *ix*

Acknowledgments   *xiii*

PART ONE
SETTING THE CONTEXTS

Chapter 1: The Introduction   3

Chapter 2: A Framework for Looking at Learning   6

Chapter 3: Leadership and Learning in a Time of Decline   10

PART TWO
LEADERS WHO LEARN

Chapter 4: Tom's Case   17

Chapter 5: Commentary on Tom's Case   31

    Tom's Starting Points   32
    Tom Examines His Practice   33
    Tom Makes New Sense   34
    Tom Translates His Learning   34
    Tom Takes New Action   35

Chapter 6: Paul's Case   37

Chapter 7: Commentary on Paul's Case   53

      Paul's Starting Points   54
      Paul Makes New Sense   56
      Paul Takes New Action   57
      Conclusion to Part Two   60

                        PART THREE
              HOW LEADERS LEARN

Chapter 8: Steve's Case   63

Chapter 9: Joe's Case   76

Chapter 10: Commentary on Joe's Case   106

      Joe and the Group Make New Sense   108
      Joe Translates   111

Chapter 11: A Theory of Interactive Learning   114

                        PART FOUR
              A LEADER WHO LEADS

Chapter 12: Lew's Case   123

Chapter 13: Commentary on Lew's Case   162

      Taking Personal Responsibility   163

      Recognizing the Other Person   165
      Structuring Interactions   167

                        PART FIVE
                  CONCLUSION

Chapter 14: Re-Defining Leadership Style   173

Final Word   177

Appendix: Materials and Methodology   178

Preface

"Three years ago I was looking for no-nonsense type skills which could help me get my point across to my boss. How-to-do-it techniques, that's what I wanted," Paul, an administrator, said, continuing, "I was not looking to get 'involved.' Maybe I was fooling myself because I did get involved, in that I found myself examining my *own* behavior; I started looking at the tensions and pressures of the job, and the consequences to my health. My hopes and fears got involved as I began for the first time in a twenty-year career to . . . You know how you can sit alone in your office at the end of a tough day, or lie awake before sleep—the questions you ask yourself at times like this? Well, I began to bring those closet questions into the light of discussion. Crazy. But then, these things gnaw away for years, and that's no fun either.

"I mean, for example, I saw my boss as dead wrong, but in the quiet before sleep I'd ask myself, 'How come I get so bent out of shape when this guy comes?' Oh, I had plenty of answers, but over the years, none satisfied me."

The administrator speaking here is one of five whose case stories of learning and changed leadership styles constitute the heart of this book. The learning and changed behavior of these administrators is a testament to their courage and desire to learn, as well as an expression of the work done at the Leadership and Learning Cooperative (LLC): An Inservice Program for Personal Growth and Professional Effectiveness for School Leaders.

LLC has been in existence since 1973, thanks to Charles E. Brown, who had the idea for beginning the program, and to the Carnegie Foundation of New York which funded it for four years. The idea of writing a book was not an original intent of the program but an outgrowth of the program's work. The idea took shape during the fourth and final year of the grant-funded program activity as two of the four remaining founders, Mary Winslow and Barry Jentz, took on a new partner, Joan Wofford.

The opportunity to write a book coincided with the decision in the spring of 1977 to continue the consultation program through contracts with school systems and individual administrators. For the most part, then, this book has been written during our first year of creating an independent organization based not on a grant but on contracts.

"Write a book, consult, and start an organization all at one time?" we were asked and asked ourselves, in doubt. And, "Write a book together, *three* of you?" we were asked and asked ourselves, wondering if we could do it and if it would be worth the anticipatable cost in time, energy, and invasion of our personal lives.

Each of us answered that question differently along the way. But we all agree that we accomplished the most important goal, given the purpose of our organization and this book: we have learned through confronting the interpersonal conflicts which must characterize any attempt to write together.

Along the way, we divided the writing into three parts: case stories, commentaries, and self-help Exercises. After finishing a full draft of the book in this combination of forms and giving it to ten people to read—professors, administrators, and consultants—we decided not to include the self-help exercises because they were not validated or adequately integrated into the rest of the book. The self-help exercises were Mary Winslow's contribution. With the decision not to include these exercises came the further decision not to include her name as an author of this book. Though her name is absent, the book remains an expression of the work that she and Barry Jentz have attempted to carry out over a period of five years with administrators, and it also remains an expression of many of her ideas about learning and consulting. The book, furthermore, has benefited from her critical help.

When Joan Wofford joined LLC in the fall of 1977, she brought the experience of a teacher, administrator, consultant to organizations, and writer. Most importantly for this book, she brought a curiosity and excitement not focused exclusively on the work which LLC had been doing but on the theory which lay behind that work, the thinking about a learning process and about facilitating that process through consultation. Wofford contributed both steady belief in what Jentz was doing in practice and a form of analytic thinking and questioning that helped make orderly and rational the disorderly processes of learning and leading.

Barry Jentz's practice and thought over the past fifteen years as a teacher, administrator, consultant, and (National Training Laboratories) trainer, together with his extensive work with Kiyo Morimoto on the nature of the learning process, provide both the theoretical basis and the practice that frames this book. Jentz wrote the case stories based on his consultative work with administrators, which he had documented extensively with audiotapes and field notes. (An appendix on the methodology and on the case story as a form is included at the end of this book.)

This book is intended for an audience of practitioners—administrators and consultants—and for teachers and students in professional schools. The book is not, however, restricted only to those audiences, as it attempts to speak to issues of personal learning and interpersonal change that are generic rather than specific to the particular settings in which they occur in this book.

Furthermore, this book, written by a man and a woman, is intended for women administrators as well as men. Unfortunately, our richest data on administrative learning belonged to men—perhaps because there are significantly more male administrators than female. We regret the all-male cast of characters but take hope from the fact that a number of female readers have found the book relevant and useful.

Acknowledgments

This book is dedicated to Kiyo Morimoto and his work. That work lives more in the hearts and minds of those of us who have had contact with him personally than in the printed word. For the first four years of the LLC Program, Kiyo was a regular once-a-month consultant to us, as well as mentor and friend. His assumptions about people, learning, and teaching are the foundation of this book.

Donald A. Schön has been a mentor to both of us at separate times. His written work, more recently in partnership with Chris Argyris, has both confirmed and helped define the focus and direction of our work. In particular, we are indebted to the research presented in *Theory in Action* by Chris Argyris and Donald Schön. Finally, Don's suggested revisions of an early draft of this book have provoked and guided us in setting its final form.

Bill Ronco aided us in getting started on this book, and his questions and comments on a late draft were important to our efforts to rewrite.

Over a period of two years, Fran and Jane Manzelli, principal and teacher, read each of the case stories as they were written, and provided a much-needed check on their readability and usefulness.

Others who graciously read the book and provided much-needed confirmation and new perspectives included: Daniel S. Cheever, Jay S. Flocks, Meredith H. Jones, Henry M. Morgan, Barbara Pavan, Richard Sprague, and John G. Wofford.

To our spouses, Carla and Jack, as well as to our families, we owe the deepest thanks for their patience and support. They gave up a lot in giving us the opportunity to write this book.

Our secretary, Tina Renard, has flawlessly typed and retyped this book and also made writing possible by doing everything from managing our business to taking care of Joan's children.

Finally, we are grateful to the principals who have allowed us to tell their stories. It is a shame that each of them cannot be personally acknowledged for the learning they risked and generously shared.

LEADERSHIP
AND LEARNING

Part 1 | SETTING THE CONTEXTS

1 | Introduction

This book presents a theory of personal learning. That learning leads to changed leadership styles as pictured in five cases of administrative conflict and analyzed in commentaries. The uniqueness of this book lies in the extent to which a theory of learning is embedded in pictures of administrators in the act of changing certain patterns of feeling and thought. Expanded patterns of thought and feeling enable these administrators to invent new ways to work with people.

Each of the cases starts with a leader trapped in an interpersonal conflict from which, by the end of the case, the leader frees himself. In the process, he tells us how he has changed personally and how that personal change has enabled him to alter his interpersonal behavior. The process of learning is reported in the first two cases and, in the next two cases, is explored in depth as it occurs in protected settings. That learning culminates, in the last case, in the real-world actions of a leader who brings his learning to bear in his interactions with a subordinate with whom he has a history of avoidance and conflict. The leader's changed interpersonal behavior enables the subordinate to interact differently with others.

In short, this book argues that the personal learning of administrators results in changed interpersonal behavior which makes leaders feel more competent and enables subordinates to perform more effectively.

The process of personal learning and its interpersonal consequence relate, we believe, to people in a variety of professional settings. The particular setting of the five cases is that of public elementary schools, and the learning we describe is that of five school principals. The learning is of particular importance in schools, we believe, because the interpersonal behavior of administrators with teachers is likely to influence the interpersonal behavior of teachers with children in ways that facilitate the learning of children.

Though the cases in this book concern principals and take place in schools, the central content is applicable to people in different administrative positions and settings. The content applies to leaders generally because all leaders face the question which is central to the learning of leaders in this book, "What do I as a leader do when I am faced with a problem I don't know how to solve?

When I respond to the problem of not knowing what to do by faking an expertise I do not feel or believe, I risk feeling like a fraud. When I admit I do not know, I risk looking like a fool. Feeling like a fraud opens me to questions about my fitness for leadership. Looking like a fool raises the same questions by publicly exposing my private incapacities and confirming in the public eye what I privately feared—that I am unfit for leadership. What alternatives are left?"

A central experience of the leaders in this book is coming to recognize and use the experience of not knowing as a resource rather than a liability. Experienced as a resource rather than a liability, "not knowing" becomes the reason for inventing new forms of thought and interpersonal behavior.

Clearly, our focus is the relation of internal processes to interpersonal behavior, and our argument is that internal change precedes and accompanies increased skill in managing other people. Some readers may ask what internal processes and interpersonal behavior have to do with leadership. For such readers, leadership may involve skillfully allocating resources, rigorously defining issues, wisely reading the political scene, or inspiring through words and actions. While we, too, think these functions of leadership important, we believe that they must be communicated to, with, or through other people. All forms of leadership have as a common denominator some form of interaction. We, therefore, hope that the content of this book will prove important not only to those who accept our premise about personal learning but also to those who might be initially skeptical.

We attempt to communicate our views in more than one way. The presentation of both cases and commentaries is designed to enable the same learner at different times in his learning or different learners with different learning styles to find relevant material. Advance readings of this book have suggested that while some readers find the commentaries engaging, others are put off by them. We interpret this reaction to be, in part, a response to having enjoyed the cases and resenting an analytic intrusion, almost in the way some people do not want to discuss a movie they enjoyed as soon as the movie ends. If as you, the reader, move through the book, you find the commentaries intrusive, our suggestion is that you stop and go on to the next case, coming back at some later time to read the commentaries.

The commentaries are offered after each case in the hopes that (1) readers will, when ready, find it useful to review the experience of the leaders in more than one form—analysis as well as story, (2) the commentaries may offer a different and useful perspective on what has happened to the leaders in the cases, and (3) the perspective offered may stimulate the reader into thinking more about the biases and assumptions which he or she brought to the reading of the cases.

The book is organized in five parts. Part One presents a framework for looking at the learning of administrators and a framework for looking at certain changes in the political and economic environment of schools which influence that learning. Part Two establishes that personal change is possible by presenting two cases and commentaries showing leaders who learn. Part Three explores how leaders learn by presenting two more cases and commentaries and a theoretical chapter. Part Four examines how one leader uses his learning to interact differently with a subordinate in ways that help her become more effective. Finally, Part Five explores how personal learning can lead to a redefinition of leadership style and identifies the relevance of that redefinition to the political and economic changes discussed in Part One.

2 | A Framework for Looking at Learning

Our goal in this book is to describe the process by which leaders learn, change their interpersonal behavior, and help others become more effective in performing their jobs. One of the ways we attempt to describe the learning process is by presenting pictures of learning that result in altered performance. (These pictures come in the form of the five cases.) A second way is to present an analysis of the learning, using a set of categories. (The analyses follow the cases.) A third way is to present an explanation of the theory which lies behind the set of categories. (The description of the theory follows four of the cases and commentaries and constitutes Chapter 11.)

This chapter briefly sets forth the categories we will use in analyzing the cases. These categories are employed in the hope of slowing down the action, separating and giving names to the rapid, nonorderly, and frequently nonconscious processes of learning. While set forth in a logical order, the categories do not constitute a necessarily sequential set of learning steps.

The categories include:

Starting Points Acknowledging discrepancies between intentions, actions, and consequences

Examining Practice Confronting assumptions about self and others

Making New Sense Entertaining the possibility of alternative assumptions about self and others

Translating Attempting, in a protected setting, to invent and practice new behavior based on the new assumptions

Taking New Action Using one's position as a leader, informed by new assumptions, to create the conditions for learning

Starting Points

"Starting Points" seem to have as a central quality something that does not "make sense." Things seem to be off, mismatched, in conflict, either within oneself or between one's hopes and the consequences in the real world of one's actions. Old skills do not work. Successful practices no longer succeed. Frequently the discrepancy manifests itself in interpersonal conflict. What does a leader do with the information that discrepancies exist? What does a leader do when he or she cannot make sense, when things seem "off"?

There appear to be four general categories of response. One response is to *fight*. Another response is *flight*. A third response is to become *indifferent*, to stop caring. A fourth response is to *learn*.

Examining Practice

The phrase "examining practice" is intended to convey the idea of a disciplined inquiry into one's specific actions for the purpose of discovering the assumptions which govern action. Those assumptions primarily involve cherished truths about the relationship between parts of the self, and the relationship between the self and other people. Generally, as humans, we are unfamiliar with the deep-seated assumptions which govern much of our thought, feelings, and action. While we can verbalize what we think we believe, we frequently evidence a different set of beliefs when our actions are scrutinized. This gap between theory and practice is captured in the popular parlance by sayings like:

"Do as I say, not as I do."

"Practice what you preach."

"To see ourselves as others see us."

Assumptions are held at an emotional level. Frequently, they take the form of if-then statements which are negative and judgmental. They must be discovered at an emotional level to be consciously chosen or relinquished.

To illustrate what we mean by an assumption regarding parts of the self, let us look ahead to the first case. There we will see a leader who rationally accepts the idea that people feel fear but emotionally appears to feel ashamed because he is afraid. His judgment that his feeling of fear is a sign of failure (which is the view of one part of the self) is in conflict with the feeling of being afraid (which is the view of another part of the self). His judgment that his feeling is a sign of failure does not disperse his feeling . . . and the persistence of the fear does not soften the judgment. The relationship is one of contradiction and stalemate. Yet the leader does not at first consciously know that he has these conflicting thoughts and feelings. When he becomes aware of the feelings and fully feels them, he becomes conscious of the assumption he holds that he may not know he held: that if he is afraid, then he is unfit to be a leader.

Assumptions about the relationship between parts of the self form the central content of examining practice. Assumptions about the relationship of the self to others, while also important, tend to have less intense emotional content.

The specific activities which frequently occur as one examines practice include: slowing down the action, isolating a single action, inquiring systematically into the thoughts and feelings that accompany that action, confronting the unacknowledged feelings, coming fully to feel those feelings, and searching for the assumptions which give rise to the thoughts and feelings.

Making New Sense

"Making new sense" generally occurs when a person has unearthed and confronted a particular assumption and is ready either to choose consciously to retain it or to entertain an alternative assumption. Release and hope come with the realization that one need not be bound forever by what one thought were immutable truths about oneself and others. Different interpretations are possible. New sense can be made of old facts.

The leader in the first case, referred to earlier, can shift from the assumption that if he is afraid, then he is unfit to lead, to the assumption that if he can be afraid without shame of the fear, then the fear can be a resource rather than a liability and can make him potentially more fit to be a leader. If he were not capable of feeling afraid in fearful situations, he would risk making inappropriate judgments.

A second and even deeper emotional realization accompanies the repeated discovery of the power of alternative assumptions. That realization is that meaning is not fixed and final, something existing in the world which has to be discovered. Meaning is created and maintained by the knower. Truth is relative, meaning is made, people create their one "sense." Furthermore, people are unique creatures because they are meaning makers.

Translating

By "translating" we mean an organized phase of learning in which the learner attempts, in a protected setting, to test out new assumptions by creating new actions.

The importance of this phase is based on three central premises: That insights do not easily translate into changed behavior because of a continuing tension between old and new patterns; that improved interactional skills cannot be learned alone, yet leaders tend to rely on learning alone; and, that new behavior based on new assumptions often conflicts with the expectations other people have of appropriate leadership behavior.

The new content area for learning in the "translating" phase is that of the imagination: imagining what the other person's assumptions might be. Where, in "examining practice," one learned to take oneself into account differently, in "translating," one learns a range of skills for taking other people into account differently.

Taking New Action

Discrepancies lead to learning, learning to new assumptions, and new assumptions to new actions. When we come to "taking new action," we argue that new actions can lead to creating conditions for the learning of others. Using the experience of one's own learning and the authority of one's position, a leader can interact with other people to produce the consequences not of competition but of learning. A leader who can take personal responsibility for both old and new assumptions, is thereby enabled to reach out to other people by attempting to imagine their assumptions, and to structure interactions in ways that move toward mutual exchanges.

Before turning to the cases, we will briefly examine in Chapter 3 the ways in which one set of contextual changes can call into question the assumptions upon which leaders have based their actions and assessments of success. These assumptions are general and involve relationships between the self and the context in which leadership is offered. The kinds of changes depicted in the next chapter can lead to discrepancies of the sort which constitute Starting Points.

3 | Leadership and Learning in a Time of Decline

While much of the remainder of this book will describe real leaders in specific interpersonal conflicts, we attempt in this chapter to present a general framework for examining the impacts of one set of changes in the social, economic, and political context. This set of changes is offered as an illustration of the kinds of change which challenge established assumptions about leadership. What we call the conditions of decline are not essential to the learning of leaders. Rather, the conditions of decline are intended as examples of contextual change which are beyond the control of leaders whose lives they affect.

We offer this particular framework because we have found that leaders who are facing declining enrollments find it useful in thinking about what is happening to their institutions and themselves.

Furthermore, these changes were the specific ones which played a central role in provoking the conflicts from which the leaders in this book struggle to free themselves. In this sense, the scarcity of resources which accompanies declining enrollments deprives leaders of the option of avoiding or ignoring certain staff members whose performance they question. In a time of abundant resources, when the institution is growing and adding staff, the questionable performance of those people is less noticeable and to a greater degree can be ignored or avoided. When, however, the institution is being forced to contract, as is the case for the leaders in this book, the contextual changes can be seen as inviting leaders to risk learning new responses where previously they may not have felt the same urge or pressure.

By the conditions of decline we mean that paradoxical configuration of events—some on the rise, some on the ebb—which confronts education in many parts of the country; dwindling enrollments; decreasing public trust; growing teacher anxiety about job security; increasing complexity of forces, laws, and events; continuing inflation; and anticipations of a lessened share of municipal and state dollars accompanying the demographic shift to an increasingly older population. This condition of decline is worse in some parts of the country than in others—the Northeast is hard hit, the Sun Belt less so—and is felt in some communities more than in others within the same region. Affluent suburbs and cities show dramatic losses, some of the outlying residential communities show modest enrollment increases. Despite its differential impact, the elements of decline can be viewed, we believe, as setting the context, at least for the next decade, in which educators with fewer available resources must manage to fulfill the responsibilities of the past while assuming additional responsibilities in the present.

While the duration and severity of decline can be debated, current data regarding fertility rates and birth expectations suggest that enrollments will continue to drop for at least a decade.* It is the drop in enrollments which appears to be the major force in creating a condition of decline. But the forces of decline are not all downward. The other major factors of decline appear to be upward.

Skepticism is growing about the quality of schools. Costs are rising. Increasing skepticism and rising costs combine to produce growing mistrust. Teacher militancy with respect to job security increases in the face of both the public mistrust and the efforts to cut costs through reducing the numbers of teachers. Demands grow for a more traditional "back to basics" program, a further expression of the public's mistrust with the job schools have been doing. Finally, state control expands in the form of legislative and court mandates regarding school finance and school programs. All these areas of increase are likely to intensify as the frustrations multiply.

The impact of these escalating forces side by side with declining enrollments can be thought of as forming a series of binds, each further exacerbating the effects of the other. These binds might be pictured in the following ways:

*The United States fertility rate (births per thousand women between the ages of 15 and 55 years) rose steadily between 1946 and 1964 and has declined steadily since then. The fertility rate is currently 1.76; it was 3.2 after the war. The enrollment projection most relied upon by demographers, Series II, is based on a norm of the two-child family. Series II shows enrollments falling from 1975 to 1982 by 3.4 million (compared with the 2.4 million decline already experienced between 1970 and 1974). Series II projects the total enrollment by 1980 to fall 3.3 million short of the peak 1969 enrollment of 37.1 million children.

1. Enrollments decline while inflation causes costs to rise; declining enrollments cause per-pupil costs to rise still higher.
2. Resources diminish while demands for those resources increase both among individuals and subgroups; increased demands spread the resources still thinner, making the demands more vocal.
3. Public confidence decreases while expectations increase that individual needs will be met; failure to meet those needs further undermines public confidence.
4. Local autonomy decreases while state and federal regulations increase; the role of state and federal agencies is likely to expand still further as local communities prove less able to manage effectively in the face of all the above.

A central consequence to educational leaders of changed conditions, which we have pictured as a constellation of binds, is to call into question many of the assumptions upon which their practices are based.

The Impact of Decline: The Questioning of Assumptions

Some of the assumptions called into question by decline are those on which school leaders rest their self-esteem. One of those assumptions equates success with the creation of new programs, the construction of modern facilities, the addition of staff, the expansion of services to meet newly identified needs. In short, the success of leadership in the past was largely measured in terms of what was added to the institution. This was possible because climbing enrollments justified increased budgets, and the new could be tried out in a climate of growth. Now as growth stops and its opposite sets in, the question becomes, "How do we judge success when nothing new can be afforded, when, in fact, programs and staff must be cut?"

Another related assumption regards a leader's ability to reward staff. In a time of abundant resources, school leaders demonstrated their approval—and by implication, their disapproval—of teachers and middle-level administrators by inviting them to participate in external events like conferences and workshops, giving them released time for special assignments, or by recognizing innovative practices by directly increasing their budget allocations. Now the focus shifts from identifying exemplary practitioners to identifying new ways to offer rewards. And the question becomes, "What reward system does an administrator invent when the scarcity of resources prevents utilization of the traditional means?"

Protection of staff morale is yet another pillar of self-confidence for most leaders. In the past, morale was often high as a result of new programs and materials; the chance to innovate; the infusion of new blood in the form of young teachers or the mobility of older experienced teachers; and the generally supportive public view as measured, if in no other way, by a willingness to pay increasing costs. How are leaders to maintain morale in a time of "reduction in force," reduced supplies and materials, few new staff, school closings, public antagonism, increased staff word load, and general anxiety? If morale is low, what does that say about a leader's effectiveness?

Still another assumption defining effective leadership concerns the role of the educational leader in a building. He or she molded the educational program through curricular expertise and supervisory skills. During the burgeoning of curricular materials in the sixties, many principals stepped back from an active role in curriculum and supervision, allowing specialists, curriculum coordinators, and enthusiastic teachers to pursue a variety of materials and methods. Now in the seventies, in the face of the increased citizen demand for rigor and "basics," the eliminating of specialists, the reduction in funding for out-of-district workshops, the "riffing" of younger teachers, and the reassignment of teachers with seniority and multiple certifications to subjects they have not recently studied, leaders now find themselves expected to resume the role of instructional leader, to decide upon curriculum, to evaluate their staffs, and to take on a new task of staff development. Frequently they feel out of touch with curriculum materials, unprepared to evaluate staff for the purpose of retention or dismissal, and unskilled in confronting and working with the experienced teacher whose performances they may question but toward whom they have adopted a laissez-faire stance in the past.

In short, a major shift appears to have occurred in the educational context, which can be viewed as undermining specific administrative practices and the assumptions on which they were based. Not only are recent practices and their underlying assumptions shaken by the current changes, but the theoretical framework in which those practices and assumptions were embedded is also called into question. That framework can be thought of in terms of growth and abundant resources.

Less than a decade ago we enjoyed a time of abundance. That time was characterized by two particular assumptions: (1) that resources were virtually unlimited and (2) that problems were solvable. During the time of abundance, the critical question leaders asked themselves was, "What are the unmet needs and how can we locate the resources to meet them?" The resources were assumed to exist; energy and skill were directed at capturing them. Rarely did an administrator question whether or not applying appropriate resources to newly defined needs would solve the problem.

The mode of leadership which accompanied this time of abundance we call "additive." The mode was, and still is, characterized by the central notion that adding resources—people, programs, buildings, ideas, money, encouragement, new experiences, moral support—would produce change or improve individual and institutional performance. Many of the skills leaders developed, the assumptions they made, and the theories they relied on, were built around the additive mode.

A time of decline appears to challenge the theory of change implicit in the additive mode and requires the emergence of new organizational tasks. The critical organizational question shifts from one which asks, "What *don't we have* and how can we *add* it?" to one which asks, "What *do we have* and how can we *use* it creatively?"

This question demands a different set of skills and a way of thinking different from the additive mode used in the recent past. With administrative skills and theories called into question by a change in the context for leadership, with their confidence shaken, and with confusion and fear accompanying their increasing sense of personal inadequacy, leaders find themselves having to make decisions and take action in an unfamiliar world. They find they often do not know what to do, feel they are expected to know, feel attacked when they appear not to know, and do not know where to turn for help, let alone how to obtain the resources to pay for that help. They are thrown back upon themselves, which means back upon old skills and responses at a time when those skills and responses may be increasingly inappropriate.

Decline as a Force for Learning

While the forces currently at work upon school systems are creating divisions, undermining confidence, and threatening leaders, we also believe that those same forces provide the impetus for learning. While decline pushes leaders back into skills and approaches that worked in the past, it simultaneously provides the opportunity to examine those old practices and learn new ones that integrate the old skills with new ways of responding to change. The risks, however, are enormous, both personally and organizationally.

A person engaged in the kind of learning we describe frequently feels that he is wasting time, is stupid and slow, is confused, inadequate, and is lacking in courage and vision. Further, the norms of most organizations do not support this kind of learning, for they emphasize the need for action, not thought; performance, not learning; answers, not questions; quickness and efficiency, not slowing down to examine and inquire. As decline sets in, these norms tend to become more powerful.

Still, in the face of these pressures, leaders do undertake their own fundamental learning. In the five cases that follow, we will see pictures of leaders engaged in learning and ultimately in offering leadership in ways that seem more appropriate in the context of decline.

Part 2 | LEADERS WHO LEARN

In Part Two, we present the cases of two leaders, Tom and Paul. Our intent is to focus attention on their learning processes from their points of view.

We begin with leaders' descriptions of how they changed because we have discovered that many people do not really believe, at an emotional level, that change is possible. They do not believe that they are capable of changing in a fundamental way. This doubt is discrepant with their belief at a rational level that change is possible. Given this common discrepancy, we feel it is useful to picture learning from the point of view of two different leaders who risked learning and did change.

The consultant-learner process which contributed to the changes described has been deliberately eliminated in this section in order to simplify the stories. In Part Three the consultant-learner process will appear in two different, increasingly complex cases of learning.

4 | Tom's Case

In the case that follows, we see a leader, Tom, engaged in interpersonal conflict with Lynn, one of his experienced teachers whose classroom performance is increasingly questioned by parents. By facing his fears and confronting his part in the conflict with Lynn, Tom is finally able to work with Lynn and in large measure resolve the conflict. In the process, he gains interpersonal know-how and confidence and begins to redefine himself as a leader.

"YOU'RE A LEADER . . . BUT YOU CAN'T HACK IT"

First Year

In October four years ago, when I began this principal's job, I received a call and a letter from a parent asking that her child be moved out of a teacher's top reading group. That teacher had taught the top reading group in second grade for nineteen years. At the time, all six grades were taught reading in a three-track reading system—the high, the middle, and the low track, to which they were assigned in first grade. Kids were moved from room to room for reading, depending upon their track.

17

The parent requested that her child be moved because he was finding it very, very difficult to adjust to the teaching. The child hated reading. He was crying every morning and hiding under his bed.

When I met with Lynn, the teacher, she said that the boy really wasn't "top reading group material." He just "couldn't handle the work," and that's why he was doing poorly. So, I moved the child to the middle reading group.

I had another request about a month after the first from another parent, asking for a change in assignment from the top group to the middle group for the same reason. The parent was concerned because her girl was afraid to come to reading. She had stomach aches. She was even hiding in the clothes hamper, of all places! I removed this child from the top reading group.

Then the complications began. The other second grade teacher, the one who had the suddenly expanding middle reading group, complained to me, "I want to move one child up to her class. I'm not going to have my group increasing because she can't cope with these kids."

As well, two parents requested that their children be moved from Lynn's homeroom; these children were with her virtually the entire day, except for reading period. The parents wanted their children out of that classroom because the kids just did not like Lynn. I accommodated them, but by now I was worried about what was happening.

About midway through my first year, I evaluated all the teachers. Previously, tenured teachers were not evaluated, but I observed, conferred, and wrote an evaluation of each teacher, including those on tenure.

In Lynn's evaluation I cited the number of kids who were having problems and who were transferred out of her room for various reasons. I also cited my belief that her teaching style, her way of interacting with the students, caused some of the problems these kids were having. I said that she was setting her expectations too high for the children and that they were having a very difficult time in trying to meet them.

I called her in and asked her to read the evaluation and sign it.

She said, "I think you're being unfair. My opinion is that you are coddling the kids, coddling the parents, and encouraging the parents to request transfers. Mr. Tatum [the previous principal] would never have taken children out of my room!"

Her accusations about coddling threatened me a bit, and she was right about the previous principal. I told her she was right, but that I was different from him. In the end, she signed the evaluation.

From the end of my first year and through my second and third years, my relationship with Lynn was characterized by growing mistrust and distance. I avoided going into her room. In effect, I said to myself, "Okay, I've done something; I've put it on record that I do not like the way she teaches."

Second Year

I began my second year by doing away with the school's tracking system for reading, and switched to heterogenous grouping. This meant that all teachers would have high-, middle-, and low-range reading groups within their rooms. Lynn did not like this. Throughout the second year she complained about not being able to teach a class of such differing abilities.

My decision to change our way of structuring reading groups was not popular among teachers generally. I sensed some rallying of teachers around Lynn. Their support for her solidified around an incident which occurred at the end of the second year.

Because of an enrollment drop, we had to go from three second grades to two. One of the three second-grade teachers had to move, and by using seniority as a guide, the obvious choice was Donna, the newest teacher. However, because of the large number of parent requests for her at the second grade level, I did not want to move her. I wanted to move Lynn, who, of course, had the most seniority.

The Assistant Superintendent did not want to get involved because of "the status of teacher negotiations," so I sat down myself with Donna, Lynn, and the other second grade teacher and explained the situation to them—one of them would have to go to the fourth grade where we had an opening. I asked for any volunteers and nothing happened. They just smiled. No one wanted to go.

Word filtered down to the teachers' room that I had asked for volunteers and teachers were saying, "Maybe he isn't going to move Donna!" Peer pressure focused on Donna. Teachers were saying, "Donna, it's too bad you're going to have to move to the fourth grade, because you really like second grade. But you'll like fourth grade." In the meantime, I was telling her, "Well, maybe you won't be moved."

The whole issue crystallized for me one night as I was leaving the building with a teacher whom I had assumed to be one of my supporters. This teacher was a first grade teacher, so she was one of those whom parents had contacted with their requests for children not to be placed in Lynn's room. The teacher caught me completely off guard when she said, "Tom, you know the situation in the second grade; you'd really better go along with seniority or you're liable to be in for a long year next year." I was dumbstruck, not knowing if she was threatening me, or reporting for the other teachers, or what. And I was nervous enough about my own position to let the discussion drop. I assumed the worst.

As it finally turned out, Donna came to me and said, "You have to move me to the fourth grade. I don't know whether I could stand it being the second grade teacher and having Lynn move, with the teachers knowing that she moved because of me." I realized that I wasn't going to buck it either, and I moved Donna to fourth grade.

Third Year

Going into my third year, we had only two second grades, so it became increasingly difficult to respond to the number of parent requests for children not to be in Lynn's classroom. During my third year it seemed that I was forever struggling with whom to put into Lynn's class and whom to move out. Many parents made specific requests in the spring asking me not to place their children in Lynn's class. Others came in during the school year to ask that I transfer their children out of her class. I eventually had to say to parents, "I cannot overload one teacher unfairly with more children than the other teacher. Unless I can find another parent in the other room who'd be willing to swap, I can't move your child in the middle of the year." As parents brought complaints to me, I referred the parents to Lynn.

Of course, many would not speak to her, and usually did not want Lynn to know about their request or complaint. Like these parents, members of the school committee and central office spoke negatively about Lynn to me, wanting to know what I was doing about her. By this time I would have welcomed any new ideas, any volunteers to meet with her face-to-face.

Parents resented Lynn's basic attitude, which seemed to be: "Well, I taught the material. If he didn't learn it, that's his problem." She took no responsibility for the children's difficulties and saw no need to modify her program to help a particular child's learning needs. For example, this winter, when a girl got all ten problems wrong on a math paper, Lynn wrote, in red ink, "Correct this," and sent it back to the child. Her father was furious, "How the hell is my kid going to correct it? Obviously, she doesn't know what she's doing. She has all ten wrong."

And, another thing. She was never able to discipline kids very well, especially active boys who also had some sort of reading problem. If these boys had a short attention span, they were in trouble, because she wasn't going to modify her thirty-minute task to meet their ten-minute attention span. Her problems with kids weren't just limited to boys; girls who were under a lot of pressure to achieve either at home or in the classroom couldn't cope with Lynn.

Midway, Third Year

The evidence of Lynn's incompetence kept accumulating and even though I tried to get some of the bad news to Lynn directly, much of it simply piled up inside me. This came to haunt me. During my third year, *my* problems compounded. As I say this, it's very important to add—and this may sound melodramatic—but I'm *anxious* about telling what's ahead. It's not easy even now, let alone back then, to admit my fears. . . . to admit that they *exist*! As a leader, I'm not supposed to be afraid!

I'm anxious because I doubt I can communicate fully the terror that was in me during this time, and how I struggled desperately to hide it from everyone, particularly from myself. It was simply . . . agonizing to admit how confused I was. I was being wrenched apart inside. At that point, if somebody had offered me a job selling encyclopedias, I would have taken it. I know it. Even at a cut in pay, just so I wouldn't have to face some of my problems.

About the middle of the year, two graduate students conducted separate evaluations of my performance as a principal through interviewing teachers and having them fill out questionnaires. When they asked my permission, I said, "Sure," without giving it much thought.

The results were devastating to me! I thought that I was a good principal, you know . . . but it came out that some teachers in the building didn't think so. To be perfectly frank, I got hooked on the negative comments and doubted my ability to handle the job.

The specific problem posed by Lynn seemed to epitomize my general problems. A couple of teachers and a specialist spoke to me, "Tom, it's too bad you can't do something about her." More importantly, my professional conscience haunted me. "I really should *do* something!" The silent conversation continued, "But do I have the guts to do it? Do I? But *what* would I do? Nothing I do involving Lynn works!" I tried to think out new approaches—the hard line, the soft line—but couldn't come up with anything which gave me hope.

And then, I would anticipate the consequences of taking her on, and heard myself asking, can I stand up to the situation knowing what it might be like? There might be a grievance procedure filed against me. The teachers' association might act against me, contending that I was simply in a "personality conflict" with Lynn. It might tear the school apart. Do I really want that? Can I live with that?

I was still relatively new to the job, and there were people on the staff who weren't sure of where they stood with me, who were threatened by me, and me by them. I'd lost confidence in where I stood with most of them. I was afraid that taking on Lynn, an older teacher, would contribute to their worst fantasies, "See, it's finally happening. All our fears are finally happening. He is trying to get rid of us all."

Knowing I'd need support if indeed I tried anything, I went to the central office and got a very messy message; sort of, "Yeah, great, get in there and do it. Fine. Go ahead if you want to. If you don't want to, okay, too."

In my previous principalship I had fired a teacher. Like Lynn, she was an older woman. I had talked it over with the Superintendent, and he had assured me he would support me. The night of the school-board review came. I was making my recommendation not to rehire the teacher. It was a public hearing, and the teacher was there with other teachers to speak as character references.

The Superintendent sat there the whole time with his arms crossed, and I was left to defend my position. He never said a word. I'll never quite forget that, that feeling of being up there. It was me against them, me against the world. Fortunately, it went the way I had hoped it would; the school board went along with me. And yet . . . the whole experience was quite frightening.

I had that same feeling of being alone in this situation with Lynn. I kept telling myself it could be different. But I could see no good alternatives. I didn't have anyone to sit down and really talk it out with. So, it was very easy to think that I could just go along the way I had. "I can outlive it. I can stay here longer than she can. Either I can stay longer than she can, or I might get up and go."

These are things I didn't share with anyone. I didn't even talk to my wife about them. I couldn't say to her, "You know, there's something I should do as an educational leader, but I just don't have the guts to do it."

In retrospect, this keeping to myself may have contributed to my feelings of inadequacy as an administrator and to my thoughts about leaving.

Still, it's damn difficult to admit to yourself—let alone others—all these feelings you're not supposed to have! I knew what was right, what was wrong, and what I should do, but I couldn't get myself to do it. It was really gnawing at me. . . . I said to myself, "You're a leader of a building. You've reached a position of importance that has respect in the community, in your profession. But you can't hack it. You can't do it, and yet you have to do it." I carried a terrible guilt. I wished I had the know-how and the confidence. Other times I wished the hell I had that type of personality which says, "I don't give a damn what happens. Who cares?" I couldn't live with that. I wished I could, but I couldn't.

Fourth Year

I began my fourth year in this school as an avid reader of the "Help Wanted" section of the Sunday *Globe*. I even bought the Sunday *New York Times* because the "Help Wanted" section is bigger. But my feelings were mixed. I was hopeless and yet found unexpectedly that I wanted to stay and work it out.

The break came entirely by chance when I read an article which maintained that leaders in schools must be learners, that—and here's what really helped—just because you have these fears and inadequacies does not mean that you are weak, a fraud, and unfit for leadership once-and-for-all. Through the article I was introduced to the group of consultants who wrote it and to other school administrators who were trying to use this idea as they tried to learn on the job. I began working with these people in the fall of my fourth year in this job.

Sanction—that's maybe the most important thing that opened the door to change; the article gave sanction for me to feel a little better about myself. Repeatedly, I've continued to need sanction to release me from a grip I get on myself which says, "Were you fit to be a principal, you wouldn't have this confusion, this fear, this lack of trust in yourself."

Further, and more important, sanction was provided by meeting with other principals who revealed their feelings of inadequacy and fear about their ability to interact and be strong. This was very important—just the possibility that others shared these feelings—that it wasn't just me! Other men and women whom I saw as successful principals were apathetic, too; they had given up on ever being able to work with some of the tough problems in their schools. They, too, had hidden this awful fact from themselves and others and had trouble owning up.

Through regular meetings with a group of principals, which was run by one of the consultants, and individual meetings with another consultant, I gradually began to trust a new idea that I wasn't unalterably weak or bad simply because I had fears and didn't act. What helped me to stop hiding and to open up to my fears was the idea that the fears could be a symptom rather than a cause of my problems. Automatically, I tended to see my fears as the cause of my problem. But, looking at the fears as a symptom, the question posed was, "What's the cause?"

I could see that there was a combination of events which caused my predicament and might make any normal person afraid: enrollments decreased, there was a rumor that the school committee would consider closing the school (which did prove true), a second grade classroom was lost, there was pressure for me to act on Lynn, but no support. . . . the list goes on. Looking at these things lumped together gave me a chance to be less hard on myself. This allowed me to interact a little differently with people because I didn't feel quite as defensive. I began to *listen* to people more, really listen to what they were trying to tell me. I tried to be honest with them. I saw why I wasn't trusted by some people, and I was able to accept and talk about their mistrust when I was with them. But I didn't try to talk them out of their mistrust or try to change the conditions of mistrust. I simply brought it to light.

Frequently, I found myself saying, "I don't know what to do. I don't know the answers to the questions that you're asking me—I don't even know if there *are* any answers. But maybe together, we can come up with a solution that neither of us would think of independently." This behavior differed from the way I had acted in the past—when I had felt required to have the answer or at least to give the impression that I did.

I began getting positive feedback from people, and I allowed myself to *feel* this positive feedback. My talks with other principals in the group helped me to do that. In addition to discussing problems, we talked a great deal about relishing the positive feelings that could come from doing what a person does well. There was a connection between allowing myself to take pride and feel good and the increasing amount of positive feedback I got from the faculty.

I began to feel less threatened, more objective, and more trusting in identifying the staff members who trusted me and those who did not. I could sense myself gaining confidence. I enjoyed telling people what was happening to me and how good I felt about myself.

Midway, Fourth Year

By late December, I started thinking, "Now's the time that you ought to face Lynn. You can handle it." I made a commitment to myself that, "Damn it, I'm going to do it." I wasn't sure exactly how, but I was going to do it. I didn't have the know-how yet, but I was gaining confidence.

As I began talking about Lynn with the consultant I met with individually, I also talked with the principals in the group. A couple of principals talked about their difficulty with evaluating tenured teachers. For the first couple of months—September until December—I said nothing specific about Lynn, but then I said, "Yeah, I have a problem, too," and I explained it.

One principal in the group said, "How come you've never moved on it before?" I remember looking at him and saying, "I don't know. Maybe I didn't feel I had the guts. But I think I'm going to do it now." I remember several of the principals turning and looking at me like, "You're really going to do it?" I said, "Yeah, I think I'm going to do it."

I started seeking other people's opinions about how to do it. And I told my superintendent I was going to do it. I knew he would not forget. He would call me on it: "Did you do it? When are you going to do it?" This was another step in committing myself to action.

"Going public" with the commitment was quite important. To say to myself, "I'll do it," is one thing; I can always rationalize my way out. But to say it to somebody else out loud—to my peers and then to the Superintendent—was a big, big step.

Once I had made that commitment, I started to get panicky because I had made the commitment to peers without really knowing how I was going to do it. You know, it was like making a promise to someone and not knowing how you are going to keep that promise.

I knew I would rely on the consultant and the principals group. The consultant asked me again and again to do two things that were scary but useful. Both things involved role play. I'd always seen this as a hokey exercise, but gradually came to use it effectively. He asked me not *to talk about* what I hoped to do with Lynn but *to do* in a role play exactly what I *would* say if I had to speak to her, right now. Then, after I role-played, he asked me to talk about what had been going on in my mind and feelings which I hadn't said to Lynn in the role play.

This role playing was hard, because I had to keep facing how often I hedged and fudged and sent double messages. Not on purpose, but because in my silent thoughts I was thinking—watch out, be careful, don't hurt her. The more I had to examine that thought, the more I saw that under this was the assumption that she was too weak and fragile to hear the bad news I'd kept from her. "Was she?" I asked myself explicitly, for the first time.

More devastating, though, was seeing that what was really going on was that *I* was afraid of losing control. If I told her the bad news, she might scream at me or cry, and then what?! The consultant would say, "Okay, she's screaming at you," and he would scream, "You coddle the kids and kowtow to parents! You're a fraud with all that talk about listening to parents! What about teachers? When have you ever backed me? When?!"

Then he, the consultant, would stop playing the part of Lynn and ask me, "What would you do, Tom?" My worst fear was that I'd give in. Not stand my ground, behind my own convictions. I'd say to the teacher, "Okay, okay, I'll back you." And then the consultant would ask, "If you responded that way, what would be the consequence for you, for Lynn?" I'll tell you, this was a path of frightening inquiry. We traveled a lot of ground. The result is that I am less afraid, less ashamed of my fears, and more capable of standing my ground—I hope.

Even more difficult was a second but similar exercise I did with the consultant. He role-played me, and I was Lynn. What would it be like to be on the receiving end? That was the grueling question. The answer was that I found out how differently I felt depending on how the consultant acted my role. Sometimes I found myself angry, furious with the unfair and even cruel treatment. Other times, I was hurt and angry but saw myself as treated decently. In short, I found that different ways of speaking had very different consequences to a listener. This supported but deepened what I already knew and raised some old questions: "Did I really give a damn about how she felt and thought? Why should I? Wasn't it her professional responsibility to shape up or ship out?! Could I be negative *and* helpful, an evaluator and supervisor at once?" These questions were troubling.

As I said, I relied on the group of principals as well as the consultant, even though the principals weren't really giving me the kind of thought-provoking skill-development help I just talked about. They were more the hard-liner type—"Take a hard line, Tom; you've got to stand up and be strong!" The group leader was helpful, but the other principals seemed set on giving me advice; they were often off the mark. Still, they were going through this with me. I had that sense that they were pulling for me, and that was helpful.

Two things I did get from the group. I got the idea of separating what I hoped to do with Lynn into parts or stages, instead of proceeding in the slam-bang, one-shot, one-way (here's the bad news do something about it) approach I had four years before when I visited Lynn's class, wrote the evaluation, and had her in to talk and sign it. Now, the idea was to avoid dumping bad news and running away. If Lynn and I were going to make headway, it had to be a two-way process where the conflict brought us together rather than forced us apart.

Second, the consultant for that group, who was different from the one I met with individually, helped me unravel my thoughts about caring, and this helped me feel less vulnerable to guilt. I'd always thought that caring meant protecting others from negative information about their performance. You know, caring meant—not hurting. Any action which resulted in the other person feeling hurt was an uncaring action.

The consultant said that maybe the opposite of caring was indifference. That threw this whole caring business into a different light. Then, not giving the negative information can be a statement in action of indifference, not a statement of caring. The hurt which a teacher might feel when I give negative information is a consequence of my caring, not evidence that I did not care. I began to think that I had overprotected teachers, keeping information from them which they needed to make informed choices. How could Lynn, for example, make a choice about learning to teach differently, if she did not have information about what was wrong? Certainly, that wasn't all she needed, but it was a necessary start.

This new way of thinking about caring helped because, as I said earlier, I had not told Lynn about all the parents who did not want their children in her room, about her bad reputation in the system. I had kept much of this information to myself, and, in effect, had taken total responsibility for what I now was seeing as information she had a right to and needed. I began to think about how to sit down with her in a first session and put in front of her the information I'd withheld.

March, Fourth Year

Before my first meeting with Lynn, I was so anxious I wasn't sure what would come out of my mouth. Fortunately, I didn't begin by blaming her for what she had not done to improve her teaching, as I had four years before. I began by talking about what *I* hadn't done. That was a hopeful switch!

I said, "I have a problem. Each year I've been here, except for the first, between ten and twenty parents have requested that their children not be placed in your classroom. I have kept this from you, and I apologize for that. I'm not sure why I did; I think it was to protect you, but I don't think I did you any service by shielding you."

There was silence. I continued, "I'm not sure what I'm going to do about it right now. It's important that you know that the situation exists, and that I've already received requests for kids not to be in your classroom next year."

"I don't know what to say," she said, and then asked, "Have they given any reasons?" I replied, "I'm sure you're aware that you have a reputation in this neighborhood—some of which is probably exaggerated. Parents tell their friends, 'Gee, don't get that teacher. My kid had a bad time with her.' A lot of people who are requesting that their children not be in your room have never met you, but they have heard about you. You're in a neighborhood district, and it's bound to happen; rightly or wrongly, it happens."

She acknowledged that, and I said, "Some of it you probably don't deserve, but I think you are responsible for some of it. You've had problems in the past; we both know that. How many students have I had to transfer from your room?"

"Well, yes," she said, "but in the past that never would have happened because Mr. Tatum would not have transferred a child at the parents' request."

"That's true," I answered, "though I don't know if parents would have gone to him with a complaint anyway. But they did come to me, and I chose to move the kids because of my concern for their unhappiness and lack of learning. Also," I went on, "I think you should be aware that each spring when I go before the school board, I'm certain of getting questions about two teachers—R.Q. (an alcoholic) and you." She was shocked again. "Obviously," I went on, "people are not just coming to me; they're also going to the school board members."

"You mean they put me in the same category as R.Q.?" she asked, and I nodded. We were silent. Finally, Lynn said, "I don't know what to say."

"Let's not say anything now," I told her. "But next Friday I would like to talk with you again. In the meantime, will you be thinking about the problem and solutions to it? I will do that, too. Next Friday we'll see what we can come up with."

I felt very good about what had taken place. I'd done it. And I knew I'd handled it well. I had begun to transfer responsibility for this information from me to her. Now it was shared. So I felt a sense of personal satisfaction for a couple of things. First of all, I felt good about myself professionally. I'm a trained administrator, and I had finally performed like one. Second, I felt good because I had been honest with the teacher. I gave her negative feedback. That had always been difficult for me to do. This time, I was able to do it in such a way that she didn't shout at me and she didn't cry. I didn't shout and I didn't cry, either.

As I looked toward the second session with Lynn, I was concerned about her tendency to be reticent. She holds a lot in. She talks very little with other members of the staff. After talking with the consultant, I decided it was important to encourage her to express how she felt about what was happening. I hoped to start a dialogue in which we both attempted to understand the other's position. And I also had a solution to present to her: a sixth grade position had opened up, and I thought Lynn might be better there than in the second grade.

On Friday, I asked Lynn how she felt about the situation. "Do you want me to say how I really feel?" she asked, "Or do you want me to say what you want to hear?" I said, "Be honest with me, Lynn. I don't expect that you are thrilled about what we've been going over. I'm sure you must have some feelings about it." She said, "Well, yes, I do." There was silence. I asked her another question, a leading question, and she didn't volunteer anything. I was very disappointed that she couldn't say more. I had hoped to get her more involved, to talk about what she was actually thinking.

Finally, I asked her, "Have you come up with any ideas about what we might do to solve the problem?" "No, I can't think of anything," she said. "I don't know what to do. Have you thought of anything?"

"Well, yes," I said. "I would like you to consider moving to grade six next year. I've thought of this for a number of reasons. For one thing, you're interested in writing and history. You might be able to do more with these subjects with sixth grade children. Second, I think you're in a rut in the second grade. Your expectations are too high for second graders but might be more appropriate for sixth graders. And third, the present sixth grade teachers have very little background in teaching children with reading problems. Your background in dealing primarily with word-attack skills might be helpful there."

The suggestion seemed to catch her off guard. I believe she had been thinking that I was going to ask her to consider retiring, or that I might even fire her. She said, "I never thought of teaching sixth grade. I don't even know what I'd do with sixth graders."

I replied that I thought that she could handle it. "Sixth grade kids are able to do a lot more independent work, and you encourage kids to work independently. You also might not have as many problems with parents, because they are not usually as concerned about the same kinds of things with an eleven- or twelve-year-old child as they are with a six- or seven-year-old child. An older child might complain about a teacher, but he's not going to hide under the bed."

"Well, that's true," she said. I tried to get her to react to my suggestion, but she had difficulty. So I continued, "That's what I've been considering. I'd like you to think about it, too, and come back to talk again next Friday."

"Another meeting? Is it really necessary?" she asked. "Yes, it is," I said.

The week after the second session, I learned that after each of our discussions, Lynn had reported them to a teacher with whom she shared a planning period. The teacher Lynn spoke to said that after the first session, Lynn was very angry. She asked, "Do you think Tom's fair? Has Tom always been fair with you?" The teacher replied that she always felt I'd been fair with her. "Very fair; in fact, more than fair."

After reporting this, the teacher asked me what was going on. I said, "I'd rather not get into it right now, because I'm meeting with Lynn again." After the second session, Lynn saw the same teacher, who later said to me, "You saw Lynn today, huh? She was all upset."

As I pointed out earlier, Lynn isn't close to anybody on the staff. She's a loner and has few people to talk with about her feelings. So, I was glad she could at least say something to that teacher.

On Friday of the third week, I was scheduled to see Lynn again. That morning I was in the teachers' room during recess, and Lynn was there. She came over to me, appearing very friendly, and said, "Tom, I've been thinking over what you said, and I've decided I'll go over to grade six. But I might need some help." I said, "Well, sure, we'll give you all the help you need. I hope you'll be able to spend some time visiting in the sixth grade rooms to get a feel for what they're going through. Why don't we talk about it more this afternoon?"

"Oh, I don't think we have to meet again because I just told you that I'm all set to go," Lynn said quickly.

"But I'd just like to talk it over with you," I replied.

"I don't think we have any more to talk about," Lynn emphasized. "I've made up my mind. It's all over. I'll go."

She caught me off guard, because I was getting ready for our one o'clock meeting. So, we didn't have that third meeting. We've talked a bit in the hallway, and in the teachers' room, but I haven't had another formal meeting with her.

One of the consultants thinks that I ought to, but I am not convinced that it's the best thing to do right now. The consultant thinks that I may still have problems with parents of Lynn's students and that I might be forced to take some type of action to dismiss her. Moreover, by not putting it in writing, Lynn is in a position to say, "I didn't want to go; he made me go; I was succeeding where I was."

In many ways, I'm very satisfied with the way things are right now. I know Lynn is timid about going to grade six, but the fear has not paralyzed her.

She has already asked to visit a sixth grade class. I told her I was pleased and hoped she'd spend more than one day there.

When I told the sixth grade teachers what was going on, one of them, an older woman, a traditional teacher and a good one, called Lynn at home. "Tom told me you were coming to grade six," she said, "and I just wanted to let you know that I'm eager to work with you. I'll share all my materials with you. Anything I can do to help you, let me know."

She told me she had called Lynn and said she hoped I wasn't angry. I said, "Angry? I'm glad that you'd do that on your own. I'm sure it meant a lot to Lynn, and I appreciate your calling her."

That's where we stand now. I let the Superintendent know, and he seemed quite pleased that he hadn't received a grievance and that I had worked it out. I think he also sensed how pleased I was with myself. In the meantime, the word about my success got out. The director of English has been seeking my counsel about a problem she has with one of her people.

Finally, in retrospect, I think about what was crucial to my resolving the problem: shifting part of the responsibility for the problem by sharing it with Lynn. I couldn't have done that without talking it through, thinking out loud, and coming to the realization that the problem was something that we both shared and had to resolve together. I feel very strongly that the support I got from the consultant and from the group was absolutely essential. Without their encouragement, I wouldn't have gone through with it. Although remembering and recording the first part of my experience was very painful, I take some delight and pride in telling about its resolution.

5 | Commentary on Tom's Case

The reader will have his own interpretation of what happened to Tom in the preceding story. While the authors believe that there are a variety of valid interpretations of Tom's experience, we also have our own views. The following commentary presents our interpretation of what happened to Tom.

The categories from which we view Tom's experience include the following:

Starting Points Instead of fighting or fleeing the discrepancies, Tom chooses to use them as the starting points in his learning.

Examining Practice By looking closely at his behavior, Tom discovers and explores some fundamental assumptions about himself and others.

Making New Sense As Tom confronts old assumptions, new ways of interpreting the world emerge.

Translating Tom seeks to translate his new meanings into new interpersonal behavior.

Taking New Action Tom begins to use his own learning experience and his leadership position to interact differently and more effectively with Lynn in ways that attempt to create the conditions for learning.

At the outset we should note the ways in which decline (Chapter 3) has altered the context of Tom's leadership. These ways are not immediately apparent to him as contributing forces, influencing what he is experiencing, but they include:

A loss of a second-grade classroom due to falling enrollments

Rumors about school closings

Increased pressure to take action on Lynn though her seniority protected her

Reluctance of the school administration to support him due to the state of negotiations

An increase in parental demand which inferentially could be related to decline

These forces serve generally to undermine Tom's confidence, even though he is relatively unaware of them as separate from his own growing confusion. His early inability to recognize and separate the external forces from his internal sense of inadequacy further compounds his problems, as he assumes personal responsibility not only for his own feelings but for events in the outside world.

How does this tangle begin to get unraveled? Let us look closely at where Tom starts to learn.

Tom's Starting Points

The question which people interested in learning frequently ask is, "How does one begin?" If learning in the sense we describe in this book is going to be undertaken, where are the starting points? Tom indicates that the starting point with him is the receipt of the two separate evaluations of his performance. Had those evaluations not had negative parts, it is quite possible that Tom would not have inquired into his own practice or undertaken the learning that contributes to his success in breaking his conflict with Lynn.

But juxtapose Tom's sense of confidence at the end with how dismayed he feels about the events which prove to be his starting points:

"The results were devastating to me."

"I'd lost confidence in where I stood . . ."

"These are things I didn't share with anyone."

"I carried a terrible guilt."

"It's not easy even now . . . to admit my fears."

"I doubt I can communicate fully the terror that was in me during this time."

Tom's experience in feeling his world fall apart as he begins on his own learning appears to us to be universal. This kind of fundamental learning is accompanied by a central irony: That which gives hope of change is recognized as evidence of hopelessness. That which provides the starting point for learning is what our reflexes attempt to deny and hide.

Some of the forms that denial and hiding take include the responses of fight and flight. Tom fights for his view of the problem between him and Lynn, a view which holds that the problem is Lynn's. Tom considers flight when he gives "serious consideration" to leaving the profession. A third response is to become indifferent, to stop caring. Tom wishes he could become indifferent, but cannot. When he seeks help, Tom shifts from responses of denial and avoidance and seeks to learn.

Tom Examines His Practice

Once Tom faces and overcomes his wish to fight, flee, or become indifferent, the focus of his efforts is on examining what he actually, specifically does; exploring what thoughts and feelings accompany his actions; and discovering the assumptions he holds which inform his thoughts, feelings, and actions. Thus, the fact that Tom *assumes* leaders should have all the answers becomes clear to him as he explores his *thoughts* that he is weak and a fraud because he *feels* incapable of knowing how to confront Lynn. He says to himself:

"Were you fit to be a principal, you wouldn't have this confusion, this fear, this lack of trust in yourself."

As long as he holds this assumption, he will continue to feel trapped because he is, indeed, both a principal *and* confused, fearful, and mistrusting of himself.

Tom is able to unearth this assumption because he risks sharing the feelings and thoughts he shouldn't have with others who recognize and share their similar vulnerabilities, "their feelings of inadequacy and fear." The consequence is a legitimizing of the fears themselves. That is, the fears which were felt as a liability, as a sign of inalterable weakness, begin to become a resource, granting Tom membership in the human race: ". . . that I wasn't alone! That maybe others share these feelings . . . gave me a sense of relief."

Tom's new perspective, that he is a member of a human community, releases him to think in a new way: "to be less hard on myself." Legitimizing his fears allows Tom to bring them from the forbidden back room of his mind into a living room where friends gather. He has granted himself access to what was there but inaccessible. Now he can address his fears more as facts, as new information which, however painful, can be examined and reflected on in a further search for the assumptions about self and setting which have kept his "fears" off-limits and contributed to incapacitating him.

Tom Makes New Sense

Tom's willingness to reveal his "fears" and have them legitimized results first in his discovering the old assumption which keeps him trapped and then in encountering a new assumption evidenced in this statement:

". . . I gradually began to trust a new idea that I wasn't unalterably weak or bad simply because I had these fears and didn't act."

This new assumption gives Tom the right to have his "fears" *and* be a leader. It leaves him feeling less trapped and hopeless.

Tom also discovers another assumption he holds about leadership. At the beginning of the case, he felt he needed to have all the answers; by the end he appears to feel that it is permissible not to have all the answers:

Frequently, I found myself saying, "I don't know what to do. I don't know the answers to the question that you're asking me—I don't even know if there *are* any answers. But maybe together, we can come up with a solution that neither of us would think of independently." This behavior differed from the way I had acted in the past—when I had felt required to have the answer, or at least to give the impression that I did.

Through discovering that his assumptions are his own but not everyone else's, and through entertaining some alternative assumptions, Tom appears to have learned new ways of "making sense" of the world.

Tom Translates His Learning

Insight, however, is a long way from action: new perspectives on oneself and others do not automatically translate into new behavior. In fact, new insights usually get expressed in old forms of behavior. The next step in learning to lead differently, therefore, involves translating the new meanings into new behavioral forms.

A disentangling of oneself from the other as a separate person is a central part of the new content of translation. This is accomplished through one's improved sense of one's own inner workings and through imagining the responses and experiences of the other person.

One of the first things Tom does which enables him to behave differently with Lynn is to distinguish that part of their conflict which appears to belong to him from that part which appears to be hers. This is most dramatically illustrated in the role plays when Tom recognizes that he has been protecting Lynn as if she were weak. " 'Was she?' I asked myself explicitly for the first time."

Practice in imagining the perceptions others might hold is central to translating new feelings and thoughts into new behavior.

"And then the consultant would ask, 'If you responded that way, what would be the consequences for you, for Lynn?' "

"What would it be like to be on the receiving end? That was the grueling question."

"Did I really give a damn about how she felt and thought?"

Here we see Tom translating what he has learned about himself into behavior with other people. He has learned that there exists inside him a complex inner world of feelings, thoughts, and assumptions about himself and other people. Here he works to extend to Lynn the possibility that such a complex inner world also exists in her and to develop ways of taking that into account in face-to-face interactions.

Tom Takes New Action

Tom takes responsibility for himself in a number of ways as he takes new action. Earlier, the case implies that Tom looked critically at Lynn from the outside by coming to a conclusion about her, announcing his conclusion, and departing, leaving her to struggle alone with the implications of what he told her. Now Tom moves inside the problem, taking some responsibility for it. He begins their meeting by openly acknowledging his role in their bind:

"Fortunately, I didn't begin by blaming her for what she had not done to improve her teaching, as I had four years before. I began talking about what *I* hadn't done."

Secondly, Tom takes responsibility for his own sense-making by separating out his information, interpretations, and conclusions—and sharing each part with Lynn. In the first meeting, Tom simply attempts to place the negative information in front of Lynn. He asks her to think about it and meet with him again to talk about it. He makes it apparent that he has not come to conclusions.

Finally, although he does not succeed in getting Lynn to respond, Tom does take responsibility for attempting to involve her in arriving at a conclusion. The importance of shared conclusions seems to emerge for Tom as he shifts from believing (and acting upon the belief) that he must have all the answers himself to beginning to understand that, as a leader, he does not have to have all the answers. Knowing he does not possess the answers suggests the importance of involving others in coming to them.

Conclusion

In the first case we have seen Tom move from a starting sense that something was "off" between him and his setting, to examining himself within that setting, to making new meanings, to translating what he has learned into new behavior, and to taking new action. We have also briefly examined five phases of learning: Starting Points, Examining Practice, Making New Sense, Translating, and Taking New Action.

6 | Paul's Case

In the case that follows Paul begins in much the same place as Tom did; he believed that as a leader he needed to "be in control," that good leadership involved being right, having the answers. During the course of the story, Paul shifts from definitions of leadership as control to definitions of leadership as learning and he, like Tom, gains confidence in himself as he does so. Paul, however, goes further in his actions and in making new sense. Paul becomes more knowledgeable than Tom about the content and process of his own learning and is articulate about that knowledge. Finally, Paul is different from Tom in that Paul uses his learning in a number of settings—with a superior, with a parent, and with a teacher.

"YOU MIGHT TRY LEARNING, EVEN AT FIFTY"

Three years ago, when I consciously began to question my leadership, it was late June of my fourth year in this job. School had just closed, and most of the teachers had already left the building for another year. I wanted to get out of there, too, but I found myself lingering around. It was one of those hot, humid days, much too hot to be there. But I roamed the halls, then sat alone in my office. I couldn't remember the last time I'd sat alone in my office, doing nothing.

My school was at a positive plateau. I'd accomplished much of what I'd set out to do. Then, all of a sudden, I'm "there," you know, in a kind of limbo, asking, "What next?" I remember saying to myself, "Paul, you've got that old gypsy feeling. Done it all here; might as well go someplace else."

At the same time, though, I realized that in less than a year I'd be fifty years old. . . . Fifty years old. Somehow, the fact of my age—Don't they talk about an age-fifty life crisis?—seemed to counter that old gypsy feeling in me. That gypsy's moved me every five years or so to a different school system—first from teaching to a principalship, then to a central office job, and finally back to the principalship, where I still am.

As I sat alone in my office three years ago, sweating in the heat, listening to the gypsy in me say, "Move on," I had a new thought which countered the gypsy feeling. I was admitting to myself, "I'm very involved in this school; maybe there's more to do right here." To say the least, I was torn.

June heat became July heat, and I continued to be torn. Other personal problems came up, and as the fall approached, my ulcer began to bleed. I had to be operated on. I got depressed. When I returned to school in late December, I was in the worst depression of my life.

I returned to a school which was finally in the full grip of the mid-seventies squeeze. All the teachers in my building were on tenure. There was no new blood to infuse excitement, generate new approaches to old problems. There were, in addition, fewer resources in people, programs, and money, with still more individuals and groups from the school and community fighting for their piece of the schoolhouse pie.

With these changed conditions in the school came more of what I call won't-go-away problems, where someone or some situation repeats itself, and, in effect, I guess, pushes you, pushed me beyond the limits of what worked for me in the past. All the people I'll tell about soon were like this; they wouldn't go away. They were problems who wouldn't stay solved.

All this left me with quite a few questions and a great deal of confusion:

Are the consequences to my health worth the accomplishments in my professional life?

If accomplishment means so much to me, and I have "accomplished," why am I so depressed?

Why do these problems keep recurring? What do you do when a teacher comes back the third, fourth time with the same problem? Or, when you continually get into the same conflict with your boss?

For the first time in my life I did not try to manage the pain of this confusion by myself. I made use of a consultant, and I befriended two colleagues. Through my new relationships with the consultant and two colleagues, I was able to explore the gaping unknown which lay between my belief that I had reliable answers to other people's questions—if only they'd listen—and my increasing doubt that I had any reliable answers to the questions I was asking myself about my own life and work. I hope the following three stories will show the consequences of my attempt to learn.

Changing My Behavior with the Assistant Superintendent

Several of us in the system have proceeded on the assumption that our immediate boss, the assistant superintendent, is a Neanderthal when it comes to education. Straight caveman mentality. He stands right there with a club, and you have to deal with him at that level—beast to beast.

During the years I related to the situation in this way: I'd say that if I was treating the faculty somewhat like a parent might treat children, then I related to superiors more like a child might to parents. I looked to my boss for a particular kind of support . . . for appreciation of what we've been doing down here. He didn't give it. And my reaction was to flip back and forth between fighting for his support and rejecting him as not having it to give.

We had some classic fights, occasionally screaming at one another so loud that others in the school could hear. On one of those fight days, a youngster walked by me in the hall and nonchalantly said, "Your boss was here today, huh?" That surprised me, and I was embarrassed. But my behavior did not change.

Test scores were what we fought about. My boss thinks that test scores are the be-all-and-end-all, and me—well, looking back, I guess they had come to represent a whole point of view which I saw as caring for things, numbers, and abstractions, not for individual, real-life kids. At the time, I was concerned with getting kids to come to school *at all*, cutting down on violence between kids and violence done to the school.

I'd say, "Many of these kids don't eat before coming to school. They're undernourished. A kid can't read a page when his belly's got a grip on him! And now we've got a breakfast program! And you don't even mention it!" I'd be seething. "To hell with your damn test scores!"

"You've got the lowest scores in the city," he would shout back, "What are you doing about it?"

He would bear in on particular teachers when he wasn't after me, completely oblivious to the extraordinary quality of effort these people were putting out. When I came here, the kids were horsing around all day long, in the yard and in the classroom. All that energy hasn't just disappeared. These teachers are harnessing it, getting kids to work together and pay attention. Did the boss talk once about that!

"Test scores, test scores. . . . What's your plan for bringing up those test scores next year?" he'd question incessantly.

"You crazy man," I would shout, "Take your damn test scores and get out of here, or I'll throw you out of here. If you want to try to fire me, go ahead."

I'm hardly recounting this history with pride. When he came with those test scores, my ulcer would be grinding. It would screw up the whole day, and days following sometimes.

Pure and simple—I wanted him to change. But no matter how often I told him that test scores were inadequate measures of the success of my school, he refused to budge. That seemed dumb and irrational to me, like he was a hopeless case.

This year, though, I changed *my* behavior, instead of trying to get him to change his. That's right. I changed *me* first, rather than me changing *him*. Three years ago this would've been nothing short of heretical, in my mind. As I saw it then, he was the one who was misguided, wrong. Not me. It was his place to change, not mine.

Don't get me wrong. At that time, I wasn't totally closed to change. I was interested in finding new ways to convince him to see the error of his ways, and in this interest I figured I could use some administrative skills. So three years ago I got involved in a program for educational leaders which I thought would give me new skills. Since that time, and I'm still involved in that program, my view of myself and of the way I lead—let alone the way I was fighting with the boss—has altered radically.

Three years ago I was looking for no-nonsense type skills which could help me get my point across to the boss. How-to-do-it techniques, that's what I wanted. I was not looking to get "involved." Maybe I was fooling myself because I did get involved, in that I found myself examining my *own* behavior, not just my boss's. I started looking at the tensions and pressures of the job, and the consequences to my health. My hopes and fears got involved as I began for the first time in a twenty-year career to . . . You know how you can sit alone in your office at the end of a tough day, or lie awake before sleep—the questions you ask yourself at times like this? Well, I began to bring those closet questions into the light of discussion. Crazy. But then, these things gnaw away for years, and that's no fun either.

I mean, for example, I saw the boss as dead wrong, but in the quiet before sleep I'd ask myself, "How come I get so jacked out of shape when this guy comes?" Oh, I had plenty of answers, but over the years, none satisfied me.

What's happened to me in the last three years I call my conversion. That's a suspect word these days, what with the back-to-Jesus movements and all. But I've been a religious person all my life, and I find that word *conversion* the best description, though I relate it to a personal, secular experience. I think of converting an old barn to a home. The few changes you see from the outside, a new window or door, like the new behavior I'll try to show with my boss, represents substantial rearranging which has gone on inside, lowered ceilings, raised floors, walls moved or removed entirely.

Actually, I'm quite proud of the last three years of my life. I've risked a lot in looking at myself and my practice. Though I find the rearranging that's going on inside me exasperatingly slow, it's given me back a vitality, a greater sense of confidence than the confidence I'd lost. There were two particular events which contributed directly to my changing my behavior with my boss. By no means are they the only causes for the changed behavior I'll tell about shortly. But they reveal insights which changed my way of thinking and made new behavior possible, I think.

The first event was a series of workshops for principals where I was really put off by the behavior of another principal. His handling of a situation which he described in his school was simply ridiculous, stupid. To make matters worse, he hotly defended what he had done. The specifics really aren't important; I can't remember them myself. Important was that after a while this guy revealed information about some of the pressures he was under, and then his handling of the situation began to be more understandable. He then revealed some of his fears and hopes about this situation. And though I still didn't agree with what he'd done, I could see how the pressures and his hopes and fears would lead him to act as he did. There was some sense to it.

His action was sensible when I could see the situation as he had, from inside his skin. I found my attitude toward him changing. I was able, in effect, to disapprove of his action but have a genuinely positive feeling for him as a person. As it turned out, the principal wasn't all that pleased with the action he'd taken either. But having taken it, he thought he had to defend it, or look the fool. That he could back off from his defensiveness, reveal his dissatisfaction with what he'd done, and think with other principals about how to act differently really impressed me. I had been so wrong about this guy, initially writing him off as a hopeless case.

I applied this experience in the workshop to thinking about my boss. What are the kinds of pressures he is under which I don't usually worry about? What are some of the hopes and fears that underlie his action? I mean, I tried to think about how *he* thinks about what he does. This was a big switch, because I tend to judge *his* actions against *my* thought about how he should act, as I had originally judged the principal in the workshop against my thoughts about how to do things. The result is that the boss's actions, like those of the principal in the workshop, look irrational, stupid.

This is very important. It was like a revelation! My boss's action could be based on something pretty solid, for *him*. If you looked at him in this way, trying to see him from inside his skin, he could make sense. And this meant that I was dealing with a *whole* different person . . . He's not as disconnected or chaotic or stupid as I might have thought on the surface.

Seeing him in this way left me curious—for the first time—about how he ticked and suggested a new kind of action. I wasn't enjoying my futile efforts to kick sense into him or stay out of his path. Maybe, I was as wrong about the boss as I'd been about the principal in the workshop—maybe he *could* change. Maybe, if I could separate out my negative thoughts about his action from my curiosity about what made him tick, then I could really act differently toward him.

There was a second event which helped me try out some new ways of working with the boss. Last year in the summer I worked for several weeks with the Big Honcho Professor who meets regularly with the staff on curriculum, and I realized that I felt I had nothing to offer when it got around to writing a final report. This thought—"nothing to offer"—struck me, vaguely, but painfully. It was like I was a child saying, "But . . . but . . . I can't . . ." In fact, I was quite successful in writing something for the final report of the curriculum committee.

But after the committee stopped meeting, I kept mulling over this picture of myself as at the feet of the authority, presenting myself as someone with *nothing* to offer. What I began to see in contrast was that with my boss I thought I had *everything* to offer, yet couldn't get him to recognize any of it. This polar difference stayed in my mind, because here I was again on a seesaw when it came to dealing with someone in authority. Either I was down when he was up, or I was up and he down. There wasn't any balance.

When I looked into the seesaw business, I could see that I had only two places to stand and act, at either end of the seesaw, and both were precarious. I was always vulnerable to someone else's movement at the other end, like when the boss showed up at school. With the help of this picture of a seesaw, it gradually became clear to me that I needed a new, more stable place to stand—in the middle, at the fulcrum. Believe me, finding this middle stance has been difficult and taken a long time, but I like the results as they show themselves in how I work differently with my boss.

This past year when the boss showed up at the school, unexpectedly as usual—you'd think he'd have the decency to call ahead—I was involved in a meeting with teachers in the teachers' room.

He stuck his head in the door and said, "This is not a good time?"

"No," I replied.

There was an uncomfortable pause, the pause which I always fill with leaving to meet with him anyway, though I resent the unexpected intrusion.

"Okay, I'll come back tomorrow," he offered, hesitantly.

I got up, saying, to my own surprise, "I'll come down to the office to schedule a time with you."

His face was a bit red by the time we walked the short distance to my office. Perhaps he was embarrassed or angered by my accepting his offer to come back at another time.

"I left the test scores on your desk," he said, a little flustered. "I want to be with you when you go over them."

"Okay. How about ten o'clock tomorrow morning?" I suggested, and he agreed.

As I walked back to my meeting, I was surprised and pleased with myself. "Gee, that was all right," I said to myself. "I didn't even get upset. Gave myself an even break, at least." Instead of trapping myself by giving up my meeting with the teachers, resenting the intrusion, then feeling justified and righteous in battling the boss on the test scores, I gave myself some room to operate, not to mention keeping my word with the teachers. I say they're important, then often leave them for this kind of interruption.

The next morning I led off. "You know from the past how little I value test scores. That holds true now, when they've gone up, just as it did when they were lower." We are still the lowest in the city but compare favorably to national norms.

I continued, "But I've been rather pigheaded about the importance of the scores. Looking at test scores from your perspective in the central office, I can see how you'd want some way of talking to the public about how we and other schools are doing . . . or maybe . . . how are they important to you . . .?"

To say that he was surprised would be mild. But to say our conversation was of great consequence would be a mistake. It was decent. Civil. I learned a bit about how he thinks, which I did not know before. He even said that he could see how putting pressure on us for increased scores could hurt our efforts here. I took that with a grain of salt; I mean, the scores have gone up. But still, that was new behavior for him. And I said, "Terrific. I'm glad you are pleased for us," and I was.

In terms of my growth, a key moment came when he'd just left. I reflexively began to think and act in an old pattern, *and* recognized it before it led me to feeding my ulcer. The old thought was, "That SOB is going to think he convinced me to change, and that's why our scores went up, and he'll take credit. I can't let him walk out of here believing that. I've got to do something!" In a manner of speaking, a part of me was already out in the parking lot arguing with him, attempting to correct his false impression, though, of course, I'd never left the building.

The point is, I wasn't so much in the grip of that pattern that I couldn't get out of it right then, by seeing it from a new and different perspective. The new perspective I used right in the moment was only a shorthand for a great deal of rearranging which has gone on inside me.

"Hey," I called out, silently, "You're on the seesaw." These words alone were enough to help me regain my balance. They remind me of the extremes in my thinking. When I stand at one end of the seesaw, I'm saying, "*I* know, *you* don't; I must get you to change." At the other end, I'm saying, "*I* don't know; *you* do; you must get me to change." Standing at either end, I am preoccupied with control—my control of you or your control of me. When the boss left, I began automatically to hold myself responsible for controlling his thinking—"I can't let him walk out of here believing that. I've got to do something!" It's one thing to imagine how he might think; it's quite another to assume responsibility for controlling that thinking!

Sounds obvious, probably, but the clarity—at least to me—has been hard won. I hope the next two stories will continue to clarify the kind of new thinking, and new feelings, which have allowed me to be less preoccupied with the need to be in control in my administrative behavior, and more open to learning.

Changing My Behavior with a Difficult Parent

In a way, the Assistant Superintendent pushed me to the wall. He kept coming back again and again with the same beef. And the parent, the one I'll tell about next, did the same. She pushed me to the end of my wits by coming back with the same complaint, even though I'd gone out of my way to show her that the complaint was not justified. By the way, this is true, too, of my relationship with the teacher who I'll talk about last. She came back again and again. Her problem would not go away, for all my efforts at solution.

As I see it, my difficulty with the parent overlaps with the one I had with the Assistant Superintendent. Though I didn't see it at the time, I was preoccupied with controlling the parent, as I was with the Assistant Superintendent.

The parent has had problems with her two kids—really serious problems. One kid we placed outside the school in a day school setting for help. The other one's still here, but having a terrible struggle. The parent and her husband have had great difficulties through the years. They've been separated a number of times. The wife, it seems to me, is a very angry woman. She comes in very rarely, but when she does, I can sense the anger, wound into tenseness.

At first her questions seem to insinuate negligence and irresponsibility, "How could Chris possibly be so far behind?" Then she challenges with denials of what we've done in the past: "You never told me this before." "This school does nothing for my kids!" The absurdity behind her insinuations and denials was that I've actually put in writing that her child is behind.

Our meetings always began with me nervously attempting to make her comfortable, then staying quiet in hope of finding out what her problem was: "What brings you in today?" When she finished, I'd explain, essentially, I'd try to correct her—as I see it now. "If you'll remember last fall, I informed you in writing . . ." or, "I explained that the last time you were here . . .," continuing, of course, to re-explain my past explanations. She wouldn't get my point at all, though. She seemed to simply repeat her insinuations and denials.

I'd think to myself, "What is this? How could she say we haven't informed her?" or "Done nothing for her kids?! We've gone out of our way, again and again. I've even given her in writing what she denies knowledge of." The more repeated her resistance was, the more desperate I would become inside, saying to myself, "This makes no sense! She's got to be crazy. That's nonsense!" or "This shouldn't even be going on! I shouldn't have to put up with this!"

At times in the past, these thoughts exploded through my attempts at polite explanation, "Now, don't give me all this nonsense! You should have known. Where were you last year when I told you your son was behind? I even put it in writing!" And after she left, I would spend the day tied in knots—feeding worry to my ulcer.

This kind of incident occurred much more frequently three years ago. Since then, I've put a great deal of time and energy into rearranging things within myself, as I said before.

As my inside parts reorganized, I began to try out some new leadership skills. They aren't "in place." I say I'm groping—not blindly—but I'm not at all sure of myself either. Yesterday, I handled myself very differently with the parent whom I described above.

I was alone in my office when I heard her in the outer office trying to get to see me. My secretary was saying that she would have to make an appointment. My first reaction was, "Oh, Christ, what does she want? Let her stew." I was scheduled to observe a teacher and weighed using this as an excuse to avoid the parent. A year ago I might have done just that.

But I had other new thoughts, too. Thoughts which evidence growth, as I see it. I said to myself, "This woman scares me." And that allowed me to add, "And I'll bet she is frightened, too. The only experience she's had here is negative." This thinking released me to act.

So, I stepped out of my ofice and said:

"Hi, how are you?"

"Oh, good," she said, surprised to see me.

"Good? On a day like this, when it's so blasted hot?"

"Oh, it *is* hot."

I invited her into my office to set an appointment. When we had set an appointment for the following Friday, I asked, "Would you mind telling me what you want to discuss?"

I really wish you had time to discuss this with me now," she said, perturbed, kind of insinuating that I should make the time now. "Chris is way behind, and nobody told me. How come no one told me he was so far behind?" She was angry, for sure, kind of holding it back, but I could imagine, too, that she was afraid and desperate.

I thought, "It's not that she is so strong, she's on shaky ground! Maybe I don't have to correct her or put a stop to her; I can try to see this as she does."

I said, "You probably feel we let you down . . ." She was a little surprised.

She blurted, "You bet I do. I'm so . . ." She paused for what seemed a long time before I went ahead and said what I was afraid to say.

"You seem awfully angry."

"Yeah, I am," and she spoke more vehemently. "I'm really mad and my husband's mad, too. You should have done something!"

For a moment I began to listen to her from an "old" self, saying silently, "Hey, wait a minute, lady." I felt the contempt. But I recovered.

I said, "Could we arrange another time when he could come with you?"

"No, no, no. He has to work." She spoke urgently, with desperation, and I judged that she did not want me to repeat the offer.

After several seconds of uncertainty, I continued, trying to keep contact with her.

Since she seemed to think we'd doublecrossed her, I said sympathetically, "That always gets you, doesn't it, when you think things are going well . . . and . . ."

She cut right in, excited, even pleased. There was this look on her face; she seemed to be . . . *recognized.* "Yes! It is. I was shocked . . . When you find out your son is *two* years behind."

"I'm surprised myself, to hear he's *two* years behind. How did you hear that?" I asked, genuinely curious.

"From the social worker."

"I knew he was behind—but not that far. When we get together on Friday, I'll have out all the records, and we'll look at them together and see what sense we can make," I said, getting up to signal an end to our short meeting.

I don't know for sure—you go by what you see, kind of feel without being able to explain—but she seemed to leave on an upbeat, more relaxed, I think.

After she left, I thought, "Gee, am I manipulating this dame? Am I using phychological techniques on her?" But I decided, no, I wasn't. Maybe it feels this way because what I'm doing is so new. I was honest with myself and with her; in fact, more so than ever before. In the past I've denied her and even myself information about how puzzled, confused, and even helpless her behavior left me feeling. Without thought, I translated those negative feelings about myself into explanations and then anger at her, blame. Yesterday, I think I was pretty aware of my feelings and didn't hold her responsible for them. I tried to be responsible to them, you know, say, "That's me, okay. And okay, I'm not running away from myself by clobbering her."

What I did yesterday was a whole different tack . . . evidence of a big shift in me. Instead of being preoccupied with controlling the situation through repeated attempts to correct her, to lay the blame on her, and then living out the day with my guts tied in knots, I let go, in a way, and paid attention to her.

I have to say this. For years I've heard people say, "Get in touch with your own feelings," "Don't take it so personally," "Try to see it from the other guy's perspective," and those were just words. I've said to myself, "That's all right for them; that's their style, different personality." Without knowing it, I wrote those people off.

It's only recently that I know why. There's a fear somewhere deep down inside me that the way I responded to the woman yesterday is really a weak way to do it, to give up control like that. I say to myself, "She'll leave thinking of me as a patsy." And the unspoken thought continues, "And if she does leave thinking of me as a patsy, I will be left all alone thinking of myself as a patsy. The pain will be excruciating, a sign not only that I am weak but also a failure."

I found I could live through the pain and come out with new thoughts which don't interpret me as a patsy and start this awful spiral of negative thinking and feeling. Not that the old thoughts have disappeared. But I do have new ones, more friendly ones, which say, "It takes some guts to reach out to the parent as you did, instead of taking the easy way out and putting a stop to her."

It's been a tricky business, this, this growth . . . the sad part of it is that I'm pushing fifty, you know? What was going on ten years ago, twenty years ago, thirty years ago? It takes so long.

Changing My Behavior with a Teacher Whose Problem I Couldn't Solve

As I said before, my insights and change center around the idea of control. When I think about the upcoming story, control has got to do with solving problems, all by myself. I tend to think that by right and by the responsibility of my position as principal, I'm supposed to have solutions to teachers' problems. A principal has answers, solutions—not questions! Some of my teachers see me this way, too. Their expectations of authority play right into mine. The teacher I'm about to describe returned time and again to say that my solutions didn't work.

The teacher came to me about a couple of kids who were difficult to discipline. I would begin by trying to make her feel better, saying that indeed last year's teacher also experienced difficulty with these children. Although true, the reassurance had little effect. She wanted to know what to do! So I told her what to do, using my past experience to guide me. This worked just fine, apparently. She left my office happy, and I was, too. I'd solved the problem.

The trouble began when she'd come back a second time.

"I tried what you said, and it didn't work," she said, agitated, even distraught. "I don't know what to say; it just doesn't work!"

In better times I might have gotten her some extra help, an aide or a good student teacher. I don't have those options now. So, once again, I began by trying to reassure and explain, "We all have problems like this. I'm sure it's not that bad. These boys are very difficult . . ." I stressed the "positive," trying to make her feel better. My silent conversation with myself, however, began to take a negative turn: "What's wrong with her? I've got other things to do than hold her hand. Why is she coming back to me again? It's her job; can't she handle it?"

If I could help it, I wouldn't put these thoughts into spoken words. Instead, I gave her other solutions to her problem, approaches that I knew had worked for other teachers, though I might not have used them myself. I saw myself as having a bag of solutions or "tricks" to dip into at times like this, and I simply dug deeper. The better the administrator, the bigger the bag, and the better the solutions—that's how I had it figured. The deeper I had to go, of course, the more often my fingers grasped the empty bottom of the bag.

Down at the bottom of my bag I had a final solution. I'd say, "I don't know. I don't know what the answer to your problem is."

I'd continue, "What do you think? What have you tried? Did you try such-and-such? Why don't you try so-and-so?" I'd be trying to get her to solve the problem.

While I pursued this line of questioning, though, I was also trying to get more information to come up with a solution myself. Even though I said, "I don't know"—and this is crucial—I thought I was supposed to know! I *had* to know; that's what I was paid for! So when push came to shove, I shoved at the teacher another solution to her discipline problem, carefully explaining how and why to do it.

Even if in a dark corner of my mind, I had an inkling that my new solution would not work for her, that in fact I doubted if I could come up with a right answer, what was my alternative—to show her my empty bag, turn it inside out for proof? "See, nothing here! You're on your own!" That was inconceivable. To act in that way would have meant I wasn't fit for the job.

It was the third visit by the teacher which would undo me.

"I know I shouldn't say this, but those two boys are impossible. Nothing you tell me to do works," she said, full of anger, pained.

I reacted by thinking, "If you were half-good, you wouldn't be here! A third time! Twice I've told you, and you do nothing right! This shouldn't be happening! This situation shouldn't exist."

In retrospect, I realize that the third visit threatened me with feeling inadequate, helpless, empty, and I got angry at the teacher, faulting her for bringing the problem to me in the first place.

The days following such a series of meetings were awful. My ulcer gave me constant trouble. Look, I knew I wasn't treating this teacher right. Certainly, I did *not* want her giving children who had tough problems a bunch of solutions which promised quick and easy results. But this is exactly what I was doing with her. In fact, the more she returned, the more simple, negative, and impossible were the solutions I could imagine: fire her, transfer her, move the children out of her class. Even worse, the more she pushed, as kids do in the classroom, the more flustered I got and the more punitive. This is the opposite of what I preached to her and the rest of the faculty about how to relate to children.

So, I was aware of this difference between my beliefs about how teachers should work with kids and how, as an administrator, I worked with teachers. But this awareness alone, even including the gnawing pain of my ulcer which came as a consequence of it, was only a starting place for the examination of how and why I got trapped as I've described here. To make a long story short, the central result of my learning with the consultant and two colleagues was some new ways of thinking which made new action possible.

Now, when I sit down with a teacher in a situation like the one I described above, I tell myself, "There's no reason you have to have *all* the answers, why you have to give *all* the direction . . . *Nor* does that leave you only to do the opposite—abdicate, disappear, wait—to, in effect, expect the teacher to provide *all* the answers, *all* the direction. The best thing is to use the resources available. Here we are. Two of us. Maybe we can come up with something better than one of us could."

This thinking was a big, big change, not because it was new, because it wasn't. I've said words like this for a long time in my job. But, I've begun to *believe* that I don't have to be on the seesaw of knowing all or knowing nothing. As a consequence, I get less uptight when I can't respond to somebody who brings me a problem for the third or fourth time, and it's still there. I guess you could say I take the recurrence as less a comment on either the teacher or me and more as a comment on the complexity of the situation itself.

Well, let me see if I can describe my struggle to act differently, based on this different kind of thinking. When a teacher presented her difficulty to me, I might say, "I don't know what will work, but I'll put this suggestion out which we can examine together." Often, this apparently made no sense to her.

She would say, "Now, you want me to do *this?*"

That response from her pulled forth my old habits, and I would repeat, explain, and reassure. "No, I don't want you to do that; I want the two of us to look at this situation and see if what I've put out makes any sense. Is it something you can do? Is it something you *want* to try? Is it something you think will work?"

Again and again I'd try to get my point across, knowing I was trapped but as yet unable to act in a new way. "We're different. Kids respond to me differently when I'm in the classroom, not only when I was teaching but now that I carry the authority of being principal. There are age differences, sex differences, differences in style. I know I get a different response." I'd been through all this with her many times before. At the end of the meeting, she said, "Okay, do you want me to do this or this?!"

Oh, was I frustrated. I was left thinking that she went away thinking, "Okay, I've got to do A or B. That's what he wants." I decided I had to let her go at that. What the hell; I can only do so much.

I was disappointed in myself, no doubt! But instead of retreating or waiting for her to return, I decided to go to her, right away, and try to see the problem in action.

I saw her in the classroom trying to work with these tough kids. Believe me, I saw how tough they were. Clearly, many forces were responsible for the behavior of these children, not just her. But my mistake was in trying to *explain* this to her. As usual, my explanations did not work.

She said, "It's not my fault. It's the teacher they had last year. If she had done her job last year . . ."

I had gone right back to explanation as my way of trying to communicate in making the point that I wasn't pinning the blame on her or anyone.

I thought I was at my wit's end. Here I was again repeating an old pattern of trying to talk this teacher out of her thinking that I blamed her. She was nodding, yes, yes, to me, not believing for a minute that I wasn't fixing her with a bum rap. I remember this occasion so vividly, because it turned out to be one of the first crossings of what I call the great divide between talking someone *out* of where they are and, instead, acknowledging where they are. Instead of trying to argue her out of her feeling, I tried to imagine what she was feeling.

Haltingly I said, "I guess you figure I'm thinking you are at fault for the misbehavior of these children?"

She was kind of caught off guard by that, and said, "It's not my fault," defensively; then, in a more quizzical tone, "You are, aren't you?"

I said, "No, there are lots of reasons these kids are difficult." Rather than go on to explain *my* point further, I kept the focus on what I imagined she might be thinking about this situation she was in with me.

"But you, you wish you didn't have to come to me with this?" I asked tentatively. Those are the very words that had been in my mind, but until this moment I'd never thought of actually saying them out loud.

She turned on herself, "I hate to come to you."

There was a rather long, uncomfortable pause before I spoke, trying to give words to what she might be thinking, "Because a good teacher would handle her problems on her own, without turning to the principal?" And though she'd begun to try to speak, I continued, speaking inquiringly, not out of disgust, "because that's being unprofessional, being incompetent . . .?"

"Yes, yes, . . . yes, that's right," she said softly, like she was sad or relaxing, not so defensive. Then she went on for some time, telling me about how hard she had tried to do right by these boys and they had pushed her to her limits. Believe me, she'd thought of some approaches that impressed me.

At this point I began to tell my side of things. It seemed appropriate, because she was really *listening* to me, not defending. I said that I did not see it as a sign of incompetence to turn for help, but maybe even as strong, otherwise you could only work with the ideas you had, not get any new ones. Now, even a year before, I couldn't have said that. But I'd turned for help myself and found I could learn and feel stronger, so the idea carried over.

I went on, too, talking about my repeated difficulties and disappointment in trying to work successfully with these children, and, you know, we slipped into a real conversation. She joined me in trying to make sense of why these boys acted as they did, in analyzing why certain approaches failed, and in trying to come up with things neither of us had tried. The whole tone was different. I wasn't at fault. She wasn't at fault. The boys weren't at fault.

In short, we were off the seesaw of who would control whom, and both of us were standing firmly on the ground of joint inquiry into a situation about which we were both uncertain. We were both supplying information and trying to make sense of it right there. We were in the middle of a murky mess *together*, neither of us pretending we had either all the answers or nothing at all to go on.

Before I left her classroom that afternoon, we set up another time to follow up. That was important, I think. This was no panacea, you know. Yet in our next meeting, neither of us started off as defensive or protective as we'd been in the past. I told her that I thought both children might need special tutoring part of the day, and she agreed that she'd been thinking that, too, but was afraid to suggest it for fear of being seen by other teachers and me as a failure. We talked about that fear, in much the same tone as our second meeting, with me contributing that *I* was afraid to suggest the tutoring for fear of hurting her. To make a long story short, both boys now spend at least a third of the day with a special tutor. In addition, we agreed that these two children are "bigger" than both of us. For their benefit and ours, the whole faculty needs to work together from a common plan to set limits for these kids.

More important, maybe, the teacher's attitude seems changed a bit. She is more—up. I think she feels she's learning. Actually, she's told me so. What I see coming to life in her and in me through our changed relationship makes me hopeful, for us and for the children.

I am more hopeful for myself, not because the conversion that's occurring for me has made me solid like a rock, never vulnerable to relying on the old modes of thought and action which kept me preoccupied with control. Particularly when I'm under pressure, I get on that seesaw and, without any attempt at promoting joint inquiry, I say, "It's *your* fault, not mine," or "It's *my* fault, not yours." But I get better at regaining and keeping the balance I talked about earlier. I get better at saying to myself, "Hey, Paul, there's an alternative to being right or being wrong. You might try learning, even at fifty."

7 | Commentary on Paul's Case

With Paul, we see learning carried further than in Tom's case. Most vividly in the interaction with the teacher, we see Paul acting from a redefinition of his leadership stance. His new stance allows him to imagine how the other person is interpreting the situation, and then employ new skill in articulating that imagining in a way that helps the other person learn. As a result of his skill in communicating his different stance, Paul says, "The whole tone was different. . . . We were in the middle of a murky mess together, neither of us pretending we had either all the answers or nothing at all to go on."

As a result of this interaction, the teacher appears recognized and released in new ways that make Paul "hopeful for us and for the children." Paul is hopeful, not because he has brought in a new teacher or program, as he might have in an additive mode but because he has interacted with one of his regular teachers in a new way which is productive of growth for the teacher and for him.

These appear to be the results. But let us explore what happens to Paul in a more detailed way, using three of the six categories which seem most relevant to Paul.

Starting Points Instead of continuing to dismiss the behavior of others as making no sense, Paul chooses to explore his reactions.

Making New Sense As Paul comes to realize that he fears losing control, he shifts from a need to control to a need to learn.

Taking New Action By structuring situations and trying to imagine the thoughts and feelings of the other person, Paul shifts the dynamics of his interactions from competition, control, and power to mutuality and learning.

Paul's Starting Points

The most troubling question for Paul appears to revolve around his inability to "make sense" of the other person's behavior. Repeatedly, he stresses that "it didn't make sense," that his boss failed to acknowledge the importance of what Paul had accomplished in the school, that the parent continually returns to him denying he has given her information which in fact he has given her several times, that the teacher repeatedly requests advice from him which she repeatedly asserts does not work.

In the analysis of Tom, we talked about the terror which accompanies the sense of discrepancy and the wish we all have to flee or fight those moments. Tom's experience can be seen as posing the question, Why do we hide? Paul appears to provide some clues. What Paul does when he cannot make sense out of what is going on is *not* to ask himself, "Why can't I make sense?" What Paul does instead is to register a loss of control, to behave as if he fears that loss of control, and to condemn the person who pushes him out of control.

Look at Paul's dialogue with the parent (page 44). He begins by explaining,

"If you'll remember last fall, I informed you in writing . . ."

Here he is in control. Then when she resists, he thinks to himself,

"What is this?"

He is beginning to be perturbed and contemptuous, but he still questions and is puzzled.

When she continues to resist he thinks,

"This makes no sense. She's got to be crazy. . . . This shouldn't even be going on."

Now he flips from puzzlement to pure contempt and the wish to eradicate the situation and the parent as he feels he loses control.

Or, again, with the teacher.

The first visit:

"So I told her what to do. . . . This worked just fine. . . . I'd solved the problem."

Here he is in complete control.
The second visit:

"What's wrong with her? . . . Why is she coming back to me again?"

Here the puzzlements in a question form begin to express contempt, as he begins to feel he is losing control.
The third visit:

"If you were half-good, you wouldn't be here. This shouldn't be happening. This situation shouldn't exist."

Again we see Paul lose control of the situation, allow his fear to shift to anger which allows him to be totally contemptuous of the other person, wishing for her eradication.

In none of the starting episodes of his three stories does Paul recognize his pain as no-sense and then ask why he can't make sense. Apparently, this very question, this way of thinking, carries such terror that he immediately feels inadequate and lashes out.

The terror or anxiety Paul evidences suggests that something very important is at stake for him. What could it be that he cherishes so much and which apparently he feels is threatened? The total contempt he feels for the other person provides a clue (just as Tom's total blaming of Lynn was a clue). Another clue comes in the form of his late-night questions about himself. The case implies that Paul has only two ways to make sense of what happens to him with the superior, parent, and teacher when it "doesn't make sense" (his words).

The situation as Paul experiences it might be posed as follows:

Something is wrong which I cannot right. If I cannot right it, then something is wrong with me or it.

While his early behavior suggests that Paul has only the two explanations, by the end of the case his behavior suggests that he has other explanations available. The learning process that Paul went through, which will be demonstrated in detail in the next section, could give rise to a series of steps that might account for the change in thinking which underlies the behavior at the end. This series of steps is largely inferential since Paul does not provide direct data from which to draw such a list.

1. Something is wrong which I cannot right. Why? In fact, I cannot make sense of it.
2. If I cannot make sense, my experience tells me that the situation is not my fault or their fault; it is complex.
3. How can I engage others in helping me make sense?
4. What can I make of the fact that I cannot make sense?
5. When I cannot make sense, it often helps to ask what am I feeling.
6. I have found that if I can know what I am feeling, it can inform me about what's going on.
7. For example, I have found that when I cannot make sense, I often feel angry and contemptuous of others.
8. When I am contemptuous of others, they are contemptuous of me.
9. My contempt produces a consequence that contradicts my intent, which is to work together toward solving a mutual problem.
10. The unintended consequence of my moving my inability to make sense into contempt is that I get into a bind which I find is almost impossible to escape from once I am in it.
11. The pain of getting into this kind of bind has forced me to look at my part in getting into this bind in the first place.
12. I find that the key point is not just that I am contemptuous of others; I am contemptuous of *myself* for not being able to make sense.
13. Actually, my contempt is not for my no-sense making but for the feeling of helplessness which appears inextricably linked to not being able to make sense (and of which I was previously unaware).
14. I was contemptuous of myself for feeling helpless.

It would seem than an answer to the question of why Paul experiences such terror is that (1) his assumptions were threatened by events, (2) he did not recognize his problem as involving no-sense even though he repeatedly used the words of no-sense, and (3) his unrecognized confusion caused him to feel contempt for his own helplessness. That helplessness was so powerful an indictment, given his view (like Tom's) that he should be in control and perfect, that he immediately indicted others. Paul, in effect, was trapped by the limitations of the assumptions by which he made sense.

Paul Makes New Sense

Paul tells us that he moves from the need to control or be controlled to a need to learn. Apparently he learns to expand his old assumptions and to embrace some new ones. His way of describing this is in terms of a seesaw. He talks about the importance of moving from a position at either end of the seesaw, where he is either up or down, depending on the actions of the person on the other end, to a position near the fulcrum. That middle position he sees as "balance," "not having to have *all* the answers," "using the resources available . . . two of us," getting "less uptight when I can't respond to somebody who brings me a problem," taking the "recurrence as less a comment on either the teacher or me and more as a comment on the complexity of the situation itself," "both of us standing firmly on the ground of joint inquiry," "in the middle of a murky mess *together*," and as "an alternative to being right or being wrong."

Paul appears in the beginning of these stories to assume he knows how the other person thinks, to feel justified in getting angry when the other person does not behave the way he thinks they should, to be repeatedly confronted by people whom he has treated in such a way that they come back to confront him. By the end of his case, he no longer makes the assumption that he knows how others feel. He tries to imagine how they might think and feel and then tests the assumptions that he makes; he appears to find that his relationships are improved and that "problems" stay solved.

The way Paul makes sense of all these occurrences is to imply that truth is contextual, that he no longer believes he has to be right and force the world to confirm to his image of rightness or truth. This realization, in turn, has freed him to reconstruct his confidence, at a deeper level which takes more and different information into account.

"It's given me back a vitality, a greater sense of confidence than the confidence I'd lost."

Paul Takes New Action

Paul's new actions are dramatic evidence of his movement from a stance of trying to control those who threaten him to a stance of inquiring into how those who threaten him think and feel about the situation. The two skills which stand out in Paul's new repertoire of behaviors are (1) his structuring of each of the interactions in such a way as to set limits, avoid getting trapped, and maximize mutual interaction and (2) his imagining out loud someone's thoughts and feelings rather than trying to talk somebody out of their thoughts and feelings.

Structuring the interactions

When the Assistant Superintendent interrupts Paul's meeting with his teachers (as has happened in the past), Paul is able to surprise himself by accepting the intrusion, resisting the urge to accommodate his superior, and politely but firmly rescheduling the meeting with his boss for a more appropriate time.

"As I walked back to my meeting, I was surprised and pleased with myself. . . . Instead of trapping myself by giving up my meeting with the teachers, resenting the intrusion, then feeling justified and righteous in battling the boss on the test scores, I gave myself room to operate, not to mention keeping my word with the teachers. I say they're important, then often leave them for this kind of interruption."

With the parent, Paul also succeeds in structuring the interaction in such a way that he neither conducts the meeting entirely on the parent's urgent terms nor attempts to avoid the meeting entirely. Instead, he cordially goes toward her, is able to listen to her in a different way, does not get caught in the old responses, and sets up a meeting at which time he will have all the records available.

Finally, with the teacher, Paul restructures the interaction, changing the pattern of her coming to him and instead going to her in her classroom "right away . . . to see the problem in action." Then he initiates a follow-up meeting with the teacher. Paul's restructuring of the interaction, when combined with the new, more mutual dialogue, produces a new approach to working with the difficult youngsters.

Thus, there is considerable evidence that Paul has adopted for his own use an understanding of, and skill in, structuring interactions in ways that facilitate mutual exchanges by taking a firmer, tougher stance which clearly signals the limits of the interaction.

Inquiry into another's thoughts

In each of his interactions, Paul is able to employ an inquiry skill. Paul first encounters the concept behind the skill when he comes to understand that the behavior of the fellow principal in the workship they both attended "made sense" once Paul came to understand the pressures, hopes, and fears out of which the principal was operating. Prior to that understanding, the principal's action led Paul to write him off as a hopeless case.

When he applies this concept of trying to imagine the other man's perspective to his boss, it leads Paul to say:

"Looking at test scores from your perspective in the central office, I can see how you'd want some way of talking to the public about how we and other schools are doing . . . or maybe . . . how are they important to you . . .?"

He begins with an assertion that attempts to imagine how the Assistant Superintendent might view test scores and concludes with a tentative, open-ended kind of question. The results are a different kind of exchange between the two men.

When the parent arrives in his outer office, Paul's recognition that he is afraid of her leads him to imagine that she is probably afraid, too. Released to act, he is next able to carry his imaginings of her thoughts and feelings into words:

"You probably feel we let you down . . ."

"You seem awfully angry."

"That always gets you, doesn't it, when you think things are going well . . . and . . ."

The consequences of this sort of behavior appear to be a sense of release making her less angry and defensive.

The most fully developed use of imagination by Paul occurs with the teacher. It begins with his recognition of the great divide and proceeds through four statements here reproduced without her intervening comments:

Instead of trying to argue her out of her feeling, I tried to imagine what she was feeling. Haltingly, I said, "I guess you figure I'm thinking you are at fault for the misbehavior of these children?"

. . . I kept the focus on what I imagined she might be thinking about this situation she was in with me. "But you, you wish you didn't have to come to me with this?"

"Because a good teacher would handle her problems on her own, without turning to the principal?"

". . . because that's being unprofessional, being incompetent . . .?"

The consequences to the teacher of this behavior again demonstrate the relaxation of defensiveness and sense of release:

"Yes, yes . . . yes, that's right," she said softly, like she was sad or relaxing, not so defensive. Then she went on for some time, telling me about how hard she had tried to do right by these boys and they had pushed her to her limits.

The consequences to both Paul and the teacher are that they begin really to listen to one another.

"At this point I began to tell my side of things. It seemed appropriate because she was really *listening* to me, not defending. . . . The whole tone was different. . . . we were off the seesaw of who would control whom. . . .

". . . in our next meeting, neither of us started off as defensive or protective as we'd been in the past."

Paul's new forms of action, then, appear to produce a mutuality of interchange which is facilitated by his structuring of the exchanges, and by inquiry into the thinking of the other person through imagining out loud what they might be experiencing. Like Tom in the previous case, Paul moves away from the idea that he is responsible for asserting an answer toward the importance of asserting a way to arrive at an answer. Again like Tom, Paul moves away from reliance on additive responses. Instead of obtaining an aide or extra help for the teacher, while remaining outside and separate from the situation, Paul moves into the *middle* of the problem and attempts to solve the problem *with* her, not for her, in face-to-face interaction.

Conclusion to Part Two

In the two cases presented in Part Two, we have seen two leaders assert that they learned and that the learning resulted in changes in their leadership which made them, in Paul's words, hopeful for themselves, their institutions, and the children they served.

We have also seen that the learning they experienced involved redefinitions of themselves as human beings and as leaders. They feel less concerned with being perfect and more involved in learning. They come to accept that they are confused, to feel less contempt for their own confusion, and to experience more curiosity in exploring what in themselves and the situations caused the confusion.

In Part Three, we will explain how the learning process which contributed to these outcomes occurred, and we will focus more on the themes of confusion, contempt, and perfection.

Part 3 | HOW LEADERS LEARN

In the previous section we saw pictures of two leaders who learned new behavior and experienced new interpersonal consequences as a result. They have begun to redefine themselves as persons and as leaders through using the experience of not knowing what to do as a resource rather than a liability.

What is not clear from Tom's and Paul's accounts of their own learning is how that learning occurred. This section illustrates how we believe learning can occur. The first premise we hold is that learning to interact differently occurs through interaction. The second is that the interactive learning process is enormously complex.

The interactive nature of learning combined with its complexity explains the differences in the two cases which follow from the two which proceeded. First of all, the consultant is present in both of the next two cases, and the learning process is framed by his perspective, rather than by the perspective of the leader. Secondly, because the learning process is so complex, only a very small slice of that process is presented.

Of the two samples of the learning process which we present, the first illustrates a one-to-one interaction between learner and consultant; the second illustrates a learning group in action. Both Tom and Paul indicated that they had worked alone with a consultant and in a group. The two cases which follow can, therefore, be read from the perspective of showing the kind of learning activities which Tom and Paul experienced and which put them in a position to be able to report the outcomes of their learning.

After the following two cases of Steve and Joe, we attempt, in Chapter 12, to explain at a theoretical level how it is that we think interactive learning occurs.

8 | Steve's Case

The following case presents an excerpt from an hour and a half working session between a principal and a consultant. The particular session occurs after a year of bi-monthly meetings during which the principal has learned to reveal rather than hide his vulnerabilities.

Learning to expose his vulnerabilities allows him, in this session, to present an incident of concern to him which others might find trivial when viewed from the perspective of the principal's total responsibilities. The principal and consultant focus on the incident at length. The subject of the inquiry is not the incident itself but the nature of the assumptions and consequent thoughts and feelings which govern not only the principal's handling of this particular incident but also his response to other incidents which occur every day.

STRONG AND RESPONSIBLE LEADERSHIP

"Why don't you just go in there and straighten him out!" the parents demanded.

I knew what the parents expected me to do when they came to complain about Marvin, a teacher. After all, I am the principal here.

They said he's aggressive, negative, insensitive, too demanding, not individualizing—a whole gamut of complaints. They said the kids were in fear.

The thing is, I honestly agreed with the parents 100 percent. I knew I had to do something. But I also knew that nothing seemed to work. When I talked to them, I sort of copped out. I mostly listened and tried to clarify exactly what the issue was. I told them I'd look into it, and get back to them. I guess I did that sort of to protect myself.

I worried about being chicken. I thought, "If I had any guts, I'd go in there and straighten him out once and for all."

"If I had any guts I'd go in there and straighten him out once and for all," the principal says. Face facts. Confront the issue.

This cold steel approach to leadership is based on a belief that stubborn problems yield only to greater force. Problems of interaction become tests of a leader's strength. Failure to solve the problem totally is taken as confirmation of the leader's weakness.

This is the story of Steve, a school principal who begins to see how his image of "strong and responsible leadership" actually prevents him from taking action, let alone being strong. He holds himself accountable to an image of strength which, unfortunately, ensures he will be weak. In the end, the principal begins to develop a different perspective on what constitutes "strong and responsible leadership" and takes a step toward translating that new perspective into new behavior.

The principal's story unfolds through his own narrative, through commentary on that narrative, and through dialogue between the principal and a consultant with whom the principal was working when he encountered the angry parents. Here the principal continues:

Right off, though, I thought there isn't much I can do. Marvin's been around a long time—in fact, he's due to retire in two years. He's always been the same in his approach to kids, and in his approach to the other teachers, too.

Actually, he's terribly isolated—never talks to anyone, doesn't even leave his room to use school equipment. He even has his own mimeograph machine. He's very rigid—comes in at 7:30, leaves at 3:00, within the second. . . . Marvin's got to be awfully lonely . . . really in pain.

I know what I should do, though—go in and lay all those complaints out to him. But I've done it before. It doesn't work. I can predict what would happen. He runs out of the office, doesn't talk to me for three weeks, sulks in the teachers' room. It's miserable—he's morose like a fourteen-year-old for three or four weeks. It makes my life terrible, and it doesn't improve things anyway. After the sulking, it's back to the same old thing.

Marvin's not going to turn into a supersensitive teacher tomorrow morning no matter what I do, and that really frustrates me. I think it's hopeless, and it makes me angry with myself that I can't think of a way to make some change. It's like

I'm failing, failing by not responding to what the parents want, and failing the kids, because I know they really are suffering.

One way to listen to the principal is as if he has different parts of himself who speak through different voices. The different voices articulate perspectives on his situation and imply different kinds of actions:

PERSPECTIVE		ACTION
If he looks at Marvin's history (two years to retirement; been here a long time but changed little)	*then*	". . . there isn't much I can do."
If he looks at Marvin as a person ("lonely . . . really in pain")	*then*	nothing comes to mind.
If he looks from the perspective of "strong and responsible leadership" or what he "should do"	*then*	he would "go in and lay all those complains out to him."
If he looks at his past efforts to get Marvin to change	*then*	he would not act because nothing works.
If he looks from the perspective of his ability to think of something which will work	*then*	he can think of nothing and hence feels frustrated, helpless and angry at himself.

These perspectives and the internal voices which present them can be thought of as forming a kind of internal committee. As in an actual committee meeting, the separate members often conflict, ignore each other, cut one another off, and try but fail to connect. Though the perspectives of the principal's internal committee do not yet make collective, integrated sense, the principal continues in his attempts to puzzle through the situation and to find some way of pulling together the fragmented parts of himself. As the principal continues his story, the differing voices or perspectives repeat themselves with slightly changed content:

I think a lot of other teachers resent the fact that he can treat kids and adults the way he has for years, and nobody's been able to do anything about it. The teachers keep saying, "How the heck does he get away with it? If I did something wrong, Steve [the principal] would be on my neck in two minutes."

. . . And yet, I know other principals before me have tried and apparently nothing's worked. He's always been the same, as long as I or anyone else can remember. In fact, knowing his reputation has made it harder in this situation. I feel like nothing has worked before, so why should anything work now? I know I delay telling him anything, and the delay only makes it worse. The problem drags on and on . . .

If I really had any guts, I'd stop rationalizing about the way he is, stop saying that I can't do anything. There *must* be something I could do. There has to be.

I've been able to be direct with other teachers. There was a teacher right across the hall from him, whom I told, "I'm not satisfied with the quality of this report. Please re-do it, and include some of these things. . . ." With her it was nice and easy. My approach worked.

But with Marvin, he'll just sulk—the thing is, I'm too old for this kind of hassle. He's old, too, and that's another part of the problem. People who I talk to say, "Forget it. He's only got two years." They lay a guilt trip on me. If I do any kind of punitive stuff, it's like an evil thing to do to a man who's going to retire in two years. And in my best judgment I know he can't possibly change in the most important ways.

Actually, there are some small changes that would help matters quite a lot. He could change his seating arrangement, for example. I know that would help. He could separate the two boys who always make him lose his temper. But changes like that are so inadequate. They don't get at the real problem, at his attitude. A small change like that wouldn't really change *him.*

It's amazing, too, what happened this morning after the parents left. I just hid the problem underneath all my papers, hoping the pile would just keep piling up so I would never get to it. That's nonsense! I don't even have the guts to think about it. I mean, I know I have to, but I'm really trying to delay as long as I can. And I don't like that. I don't like that about myself.

Each of the principal's internal committee members throws his different piece of this painful, puzzling situation on the boardroom table. When each committee member offers his perspective, his statements "plop," much like a real committee meeting where one person speaks but no one acknowledges it.

Even more noticeable in the monologue thus far is that when one of the principal's voices speaks, another immediately jumps in with an objection. For example, what seems to be a voice of strong and responsible leadership says, "Act now! Go in and lay all those complaints out to him." Immediately, what seems to be a voice of past experience says, "But I've done it before. It doesn't work." Another voice of strong and responsible leadership implicitly says, "Show control of the situation." But that voice is immediately countered by another speaking for past experience. "But how? I'm not in control. He's got power, too. He sulks and gets morose and that drives me nuts." When a voice of past experience talks about small changes which might help, a voice of responsible leadership contradicts by commanding, "Act to solve the total problem, not just small parts."

This reflexive countering of what appears to be one set of voices by another often results in a deadlock where one set of voices can't speak without the other's having to speak, and where each set of voices maintains the coherence of its particular position in the face of the other. Totally enmeshed with each other, each set of voices apparently tries to get the other to change. Implicitly, "Yes, but" is followed by "Don't you see!" or "Yes, but, if you'd only look at what I'm telling you, you'd see it differently!" The voices of right leadership and the voices of past experience are deadlocked and hence incapacitated.

The two sets of voices caught in a "yes-but" bind have become a single, impotent unit. Were they two separate, autonomous parts of the principal's self, they each could serve him in his effort to make new sense and create new behavior. But interlocked and always competing, the parts of himself represented by the different voices render him powerless, even as he berates himself for not being strong. The principal seems to be in limbo, bouncing back and forth between the arguments of these two different positions and unable to take a stand behind either one.

As a way of helping the principal take a stand, the consultant encouraged him to role-play the parent who had complained about Marvin. This gave the principal an opportunity to speak solely from one voice, from his image of right and responsible leadership, an image which he assumed the parents shared. The consultant role-played the principal, attempting to speak from the principal's voice of past experience. In effect, the consultant said what he thought the principal might say (1) if he were not ashamed of his helplessness, his outrage, his uncertainty, and were not consequently putting his effort into hiding these parts of himself, and (2) if he were able to act assertively from these parts of himself, viewing them as resources rather than liabilities.

The ensuing dialogue occurred in which the consultant (C) role-played the principal in this situation and the principal (P) role-played the parent:

C: (By getting concrete information from the parents about what happens which makes John [the son] afraid, I would try to arrive at some small changes, like seating arrangements, which Marvin might make.) Then I might say: Marvin is not going to make big changes over the next two years. I know that you wish that I could go in there and shape him up, and I wish I could, too. But my experience tells me that for all my efforts, little has resulted.

P: You're the principal! Damn it, do something! My kid's a nervous wreck. I think it's your responsibility to respond to my kid's hurting.

C: I want to do just that.

P: You are the boss in the school, aren't you? Can't you do anything about that lousy teacher?!

C: It's not that I can't do *anything*. I can do something with Marvin. But that something will be partial, small. I think you and I can do something, too, the same thing I'll ask of Marvin: we could look at how each of us is responding to your son when he is afraid.

P: You call that an option?

C: Yes.

P: I just can't understand how you can allow my kid to suffer.

C: Maybe it seems I really don't care about John?

P: That's right! You're definitely copping out. Taking the easy way out. I don't think you show any kind of leadership; you're not in control of the situation. You don't have the guts to tell him to shape up. What the hell do we pay you all this money for, if you're afraid to tell a teacher to shape up? It's my Johnny we're talking about; my little child is crying every day, won't come to school every day. You know, if we don't get action from you, we'll go to the Superintendent. Something's got to be done.

C: Yes, it does. It's outrageous for a small child to be in such fear. And I imagine it's quite painful for you to have to witness the child's helplessness and terror . . . you probably imagine his being permanently harmed . . .

P: Yes, it is awful for us, it certainly is. We're afraid he'll be damaged for life!

C: (There are several seconds of silence before C begins to speak.) Well, I think we're in an awful bind here: you wanting me to do something I cannot promise to do; me wanting you to look at how each of us might better respond to your son when he's afraid. Do you see us in this bind?

P: All I know is, it's you who should make things right for my child!

C: Is your child's fear *totally* my responsibility . . . ?

P: Oh, no, no—not totally, but . . . (Okay, I'm pulling out of this now. I certainly enjoyed sticking you with the responsibility. You consultants ought to get out here to find out what it's really like!)

C: You loved it, eh?

P: You bet I did.

C: I'm curious about what else you found yourself thinking and feeling as you blasted me, or in these moments afterward . . .

P: It's funny—I felt very strong at first, righteous . . . then maybe desperate, I think, like I wasn't really so strong . . . in a way, weak, trying to prove something which really didn't hold up . . .

Maybe it's not just that I'm weak. Maybe there's more to it . . .

This dialogue picture of the principal's internal struggle is, of course, much too neat. It portrays a simple, binary conflict with exaggerated voices of strong, responsible leadership opposing voices of past experience. In spite of its oversimplification, though, the dialogue graphically illustrates a break in the deadlock between two sets of voices which had, in effect, become one incapacitated unit. This break is evident in the tone and substance of the principal's final response to the consultant when the principal finds himself questioning the assumptions behind the voice of strong and responsible leadership: ". . . like I wasn't really so strong, in a way, weak, trying to prove something which really didn't hold up . . ." What the principal had unquestioningly seen as strength, as pictured through the voice of strong and responsible leadership, he now questions: maybe strength is weakness? Measured against the standards of that image of leadership, he had seen himself as a coward; but, here, he begins to doubt that assessment of himself.

"Maybe it's not just that I'm weak. Maybe there's more to it . . ."

In effect, the consequence of the principal's taking a stand behind one voice, or, in other words, fully immersing himself in that position, is not that he became more fixed in that position. The result is not increased conviction and further defensiveness, as might be expected. Rather, immersion results, paradoxically, in increased distance. With distance comes questioning of the assumption behind the voice's statements of "truth." The questioning, though painful in some of its consequences, frees him to recognize the limits of the perspective presented by the voice of strong and responsible leadership rather than defend it for its rightness or utility.

The role play has done something else. It has shaken loose some important components of the strong and responsible image. These include:

Show control of the situation.

Protect yourself, don't be vulnerable.

Act, don't think.

Act fast, get quick and decisive solutions.

Solve all, not part of a problem.

It is this image of strong and responsible leadership taken as a whole which the principal, having questioned, goes on now to explore in the following monologue:

The role playing was helpful. I liked what you said. I liked your responses to me as a parent . . . but it wasn't enough . . . and I couldn't trust it. The voice and feeling I would fall back on if I were to act as you did would be—not enough. It had a kind of emptiness to me; it was too abstract. I don't have any backup, any support to stay with that way of acting.

If the positions were reversed and I was a real parent complaining about a teacher, I know I would have wanted a different kind of response. I just feel—and it's very difficult to get away from this feeling—that I have a responsibility to do something more, something more concrete or something.

They're not going to be happy with that response of limited responsibility; I really honestly doubt it. And I'd feel I was letting them down . . . and, I guess, that would leave me vulnerable. I can't simply say to them, "You're putting the burden on me." I think it could be a setup.

The parents are asking me to do something, and they're saying it's easy to do—"You can do it. You can do it; you're the boss, why can't you do it?" I don't know whether I could turn around and say, "There's little I can do." It's gutless. It's true, but it's gutless. There's something wrong with it. There is something very frustrating about it. Maybe I shouldn't see admitting my limits as weakness. From your perspective, it could be seen as strength, as having the guts to admit my limits, and recognize the constraints of the situation. I guess one of my problems is that I have trouble seeing weakness as a strength.

And I know that if I do see weakness as a strength, I may well lose prestige. There's no question, in the eyes of the majority of people around here, how people perceive what's strong and what's weak. Maybe I'm wrong that everybody would view that as weakness, but I guess I'm afraid of losing some of that prestige and stuff. Or that respect, the way people look at me. People still respect strength, and yet, damn it all, I have to admit that the most beautiful people I know are people who can admit both weakness *and* strength. But I'm afraid that I don't think most people think this way.

People have said terrible things to me: "Why don't you act? I don't understand why? What's wrong? Do it!" (Pause and the principal begins to speak more and more slowly.)

And then I start asking myself those very questions. "Why can't you do it?" like it was such an easy thing to do. (Long pause.)

They don't have to do it . . . (The principal comes to a long, full stop; several seconds pass.)

Well . . . I guess, I'm . . . pretty confused. (The principal and consultant sit in silence.)

In this section of monologue the principal continues exploring his assumption that strength lies in conforming to his image of strong and responsible leadership. He is puzzled. He seems to consider some of the possible consequences of shifting his assumption about what it means to be strong; he imagines losing prestige, respect, and, implicitly, being rejected and left all alone.

The only alternative to such terrifying consequences seems to be to identify with the demand he hears from others and from himself: to act. But this time when the voices of past experience rise in opposition to the voices demanding action—this time for the first time—the principal slows down to a full stop, sits in a long pause, and consciously seems to feel his bewilderment. He no longer fights it off with anger at himself. Here he begins to feel or *be* where he is—confused. Until now, this member of his internal committee, a voice speaking for his puzzlement, has not even been at the conference table. The act of feeling it can bring that part of himself back to the table, and that in itself is an act of integration; he welcomes a part of himself into his internal committee of voices.

The principal's apparent act of beginning to feel his confusion, rather than feeling anger at himself for being confused, is as great a risk as questioning his assumption about strength. These two acts are integrally related. To be strong and responsible means to be in control, on top of things, invulnerable. Confusion does not fit the image. It is off limits. To feel bewildered carries the meaning of weakness. It threatens to confirm what his voice of strong leadership says he is—cowardly and weak and hence not fit for leadership.

The principal has gotten close to feeling his confusion fully, and therefore of integrating this part of himself, but he is still blocked in feeling completely because he lacks a perspective that makes feeling bewildered and weak something other than an indictment. There is still a tone in his voice implying, "I really shouldn't be feeling this way." Here he experiences a "yes-but" bind where the voice of his confusion is stronger than the commands of strong leadership, but the commands are strong enough to prevent his fully feeling the confusion.

Because the principal has risked feeling his own confusion and is closer to it than ever before, the consultant can offer a perspective which might free the principal to fully feel the confusion and, in the process, integrate it into himself as a legitimate, natural, unavoidable consequence of his past efforts to lead and his present search to make new sense of his experience:
(C and P have been sitting in nearly a half-minute of silence after the principal last spoke, saying, "Well, I guess I'm . . . pretty confused.")

C: I don't think you'd be confused if you didn't care. I see confusion as a sign of your caring. The opposite of caring is indifference, not pain. I suspect you feel that if you were really strong, you'd be able to avoid all this in the first place . . . (Several seconds pass.)
P: I never . . . I never thought of it that way . . . it comes to me that I've thought myself a jerk, even to be mushing around like this . . . weak. (*Principal and consultant sit in silence.*)

An implicit threat in allowing a feeling to be fully felt can be that the person will simply be, in this case, more confused and stay confused, permanently. In fact what happens here, and often happens, is quite different. New meaning emerges. The principal realizes that "to be mushing around like this," to be searching for a new sense of integration or personal meaning signifies, in a part of himself, that he is a fool and a weakling. As the old image of strong and responsible leadership would dictate, he should know it all ahead of time—not be confused and searching.

After sitting for several seconds in silence with the consultant, the principal comes to another new realization that allows him to welcome into his internal committee still another part of himself which has not been present:

P: (P and C have been sitting in silence since the principal said, "I never . . . I never thought of it that way . . . it comes to me that I've thought myself a jerk, even to be mushing around like this . . . weak.") . . . And I sort of wish there were an easy way out, but I don't think there is . . .

The principal's act of recognizing and asserting his yearning for "an easy way out," like his feeling his confusion, allows him to come close to a part of himself which he has been keeping at a distance or denying. By coming close to the yearning, or in other words, claiming it as a legitimate, natural part of himself, he can stop acting out of it, which is exactly what he has been doing. He has been hoping to be saved, perhaps by the consultant. Until this time, he has not been able to trust his own internal committee to make new sense and create new forms of action. Here, he says, implicitly, "It seems I am going to have to work with what I've got, *me*; I am ready to go to work."

At this point the principal seems to have claimed as his own, and hence integrated into himself as a whole person, parts of himself which he had either accepted blindly or denied. He has risked questioning and exploring his image of right and responsible leadership rather than defending its coherence in the face of disconfirming evidence; he has risked feeling his confusion rather than fighting it off with anger; he has risked recognizing his wish to flee rather than pretending that the wish did not exist. By claiming responsibility for himself in these ways, he has "located" himself—in much the same way as a man who is lost in the woods must first "locate" himself in order to find his way out.* As long as a lost hiker maintains that he knows where he is, he will most likely continue to go in circles. Once he admits he is lost, he can change his whole stance, looking for signs and making sense of information in a different manner than before.

At this point the consultant suggests to the principal that were the principal to shift his definition of the situation from a focus on Marvin as the problem to thinking about the child's fear as the concern, he might have more room to create new forms of interaction with Marvin. The consultant thought that

*Kiyo Morimoto, unpublished manuscript, *The Context for Learning.*

the principal's initial definition of the situation made the principal an adversary to Marvin. By contrast, with the child's fear defined as the concern, the principal might see Marvin, the parents, and himself all as resources in attempting to resolve the concern about the child's fear.

After a discussion of this different way of defining the situation, the principal and consultant agreed that the principal would try to invent new ways of talking to Marvin and act them out.

In the dialogue which follows, the principal speaks as he imagines he might to Marvin; the consultant serves first as prompter and then as inquirer, testing what the principal is experiencing as he invents new behavior:

P: Damn it! This is always difficult . . . Maybe I'd say, "Marvin, we have talked before about how frightened John is about coming to school. His parents came in to talk about this. I asked them to look at their part in his difficulty, and in the process they identified several things they think you could do to help the situation . . ." What if he interrupts me?

C: Tell him to wait until you finish.

P: Would you lay out the changes you arrived at with the parents?

C: Maybe. I'd try to be clear in myself if they were expectations which I had for him or suggestions to discuss. To put it differently, are you there to discuss whether or not these changes will be made, or *how*?

P: . . . You know, given what Marvin and I have been through before, I'd say, "Here are two things I want you to do." I'd explain them, things like changing the seating arrangement. "I know you think I coddle the kids, and parents, too, for that matter, but I want you to do these two things.

"Now, I want to talk with you about what these actions will be trying to achieve. John is afraid . . ." I feel good about this. What's coming clear is that I won't be so intimidated by him if he attacks me or goes into a sulk.

C: You sense you can trust yourself . . .?

P: Yes, . . . I guess if I'm not damning myself I can pay attention to the kid and to Marvin, too. You know—think on my feet. He doesn't want to harm this boy . . . I might say to him, "I know you have tried very hard with this boy, and yet he still finds himself overwhelmed. Here are things I want done; maybe we can think together about others which might be more effective . . ."

I feel good about this. I think I can go ahead and think this through on my own. If the past holds true, I won't do what I acted out here. But I'll be able to figure out something new on my own while the conversation actually occurs.

From the beginnning of his story to the end of the second role play, the principal seems to have moved:

	From	To
Emotionally:	When he began he was angry and ashamed of being help- less and hopeless. He was confused but not con- scious or accepting of that confusion. In part, his wish was to flee.	When he ends, there is little anger and shame. He feels less helpless, more hopeful and assertive. He is conscious that he is confused and searching for clarity. His wish is to learn and act.
Intellectually:	When he began, he was trapped by the parent's and his own definition of the problem. The problem was the teacher. As well, he was trapped by the perfectionistic standards of his definition of strong and responsible leadership.	When he ends, he sees another focus for the problem—the child's fears and lack of learning. As well, he has expanded his definition of leadership a bit to allow himself to act partially rather than expect himself to "do it all." In addition, he seems to see strength as some- thing to be accomplished *with*, not *against*, others and as a capacity ("think on my feet") which can be developed rather than a commodity which he either has or does not.
In action:	When he began, he had a singular response— "lay out all those com- plaints," which he knew wouldn't work.	When he ends, he has new alternatives and the promise of creating others.

Certainly, these shifts in the principal's way of feeling, thinking, and acting must be frequently tested in action to be confirmed, or disconfirmed. But in the upcoming moment of interaction with Marvin, and, perhaps, in future interaction with parents, he has this experience of trusting in his capacity to make new sense and create new behavior to back him up, to support him when he meets resistance. At the outset, when the strongest backup he had was the voice and image of strong and responsible leadership, he judged himself a fool and a coward. Feeling foolish and cowardly is hardly a good backup for participating confidently in a conflict situation.

Had the principal abandoned the voices of past experience which would not fit his image of strong and responsible leadership, he might have avoided the self-accusation of cowardice and the pain that resulted. But had he done this, he would have denied himself the opportunity to learn. These parts of his experience were informing him about the inadequacy of his image. That image was not large enough and complex enough to encompass his firsthand experience with the world in which he chose to lead. He did not abandon these parts of himself. Instead, he struggled to integrate them into a broader and deeper definition of self and leadership. In part, the principal made this redefinition possible by risking dialogue with another person who offered him ways of thinking, feeling, and acting which were different from his own. Without that risk, he would in all likelihood remain trapped in the limits of his own image and definition of strong and responsible leadership.

9 | Joe's Case

In the case which follows, we again see a close-up picture of how a leader learns new interpersonal behavior. This time, unlike the previous case, we observe the learnings of a leader not alone with a consultant but in a group of peers. Like Steve, Joe, in this case, risks exposing his thoughts and feelings, encountering assumptions, and intergrating parts of himself. But this time we see the results of that learning begin to manifest themselves in the invention of new behaviors toward another learner. We see Joe not only learn but also use that learning with another learner (Andy), who, after considerable grumbling and uneasiness, risks exposing his actual performance, and accompanying thoughts and feelings.

As in the case of Steve, the case which follows closely examines concrete interactions. Here those moments involve a number of actors. Like Steve's case, this one about Joe takes a slice out of a lengthy process. The group has met bimonthly for seven months before the four meetings which are presented here, and they continue to work after these meetings.

As with the other cases, the discrepancy which the leader focuses upon involves his unsuccessful interaction with an experienced teacher. Similarly in this case, as in the others, the problem of the teacher becomes the starting point for learning.

As in the other cases, the learning involves discovering and confronting assumptions. Here we will see Joe confront an assumption about himself, namely that if he is fearful, he is a fraud as a leader. He comes to understand that assumption not only intellectually but also emotionally.

Finally, this case will go further than the others in presenting two distinctly different models of providing help, with the guiding assumptions, behaviors, and consequences of each demonstrated in action.

Because a number of different people appear in this case, here is a cast of characters:

The group leader—experienced consultant
        Joe—the major character, an experienced older principal
        Sam—a younger man who looks up to Joe
        Andy—a gruff middle-aged man who respects Joe
        Brian—a cynical principal who gives people a hard time
        Ray—a rational, impatient anxious type
      George—a silent member who speaks only twice, in
                Meeting Number Four, both times to Andy

"HAND HOLDERS AND TOUGH-MINDED CRITICS"

Meeting Number One

"I tried it, and it didn't work," Joe said, apparently angry. Everyone in the room seemed startled. The group leader asked, "What didn't work?"

Joe related the following episode in which he attempted to communicate negative information to a teacher, Harry, about Harry's performance in the classroom:

I knew before we started talking that I would have to tell Harry some negative things about his teaching and that he wouldn't like it, but I just couldn't wait any longer. The parents are on my back, and I'm having a terrible time just finding enough kids to fill his class next year.

In addition, the Superintendent is hearing from some school committee members, and I am hearing from him.

Joe sighed deeply. His voice had begun to slow down, and he appeared more hurt and anxious than angry. He continued.

Harry came into my office with that blank look on his face, and I started off trying to make him feel at ease. I got him some coffee, and we made some nervous comments about the weather. I talked positively about an assembly that he had recently organized.

Then, I began to drop the other shoe and tell him about the parents who are sending me notes and phoning me about him. He sits there with that stony look, and when I stop talking, he says, "Why haven't you told me this before!"— almost a shout.

From here on it all goes downhill—polite, after the outburst, but no one is listening to me, and I'm not hearing him. Then it's over, and he leaves, and I say to myself, "Well, what's the use?"

When Joe stopped speaking, the room was absolutely silent. As the silence lengthened, the group leader began thinking about how to account for it.

The silence itself was new. Never before had this group of eight male administrators allowed uninterrupted seconds to pass after one of them had presented a problem. Ordinarily, someone, if not several people, jumped right in to offer help.

The group was titled "Issues of Evaluating/Supervising Tenured Staff." The members of the group were expected to present and examine their efforts to alter their leadership style, particularly in regard to helping others learn and grow on the job. Their most pressing concern was how to give and receive negative information in a way which resulted in growth rather than entrenchment. Some group members presented difficulties they were having with parents or superiors, but most members were concerned with evaluation/supervision interactions with subordinates.

A near palpable tension filled the room during the silence. It seemed a constructive silence to the leader, though, in that group members appeared actively engaged in trying to decide how to respond to Joe. As yet, no one appeared to have left the room mentally, in flight from the tension.

The group leader guessed that in part the silence could be accounted for by the group members' general discomfort with "show of feeling," as one member had put it, particularly feelings of disappointment, helplessness, loss, sadness, confusion. Joe had shown that he was distraught.

Still, the silence seemed to carry more import than could be accounted for in this way. It seemed likely to the group leader that Joe's past participation in the group made the members particularly wary about responding.

At the first meeting of the group, seven months before, members told one another why they had joined, and when Joe spoke last, he got everyone's undivided attention. He spoke in a formal, yet warm tone punctuated by occasional threat:

I look young [he was forty-five], but I've been a school principal for twenty years.

Twenty years. That's ten years longer than anyone else here. When I started this job it was 1957, and the difference between the job now and then is the difference between day and night. It's the night right now, and I'm saying I need help, in particular with conflict, I guess—with hurting people by evaluating their performance negatively and then having to live with them day-to-day. All this is new to me, even after twenty years.

But—Joe paused, and looked at each person in the room. I'm intolerant, even resentful, of people who are eager to teach me. That goes particularly for young people. These days young people seem to think they have a lot to teach us older hands.

After his opening speech, which he deferentially declined to discuss further when challenged, Joe participated in meetings by giving his full attention when others spoke, but he spoke little. When he did speak, he got everyone's undivided attention. In part, he did this by waiting until everyone had offered "help," often unsuccessfully, before he offered his. But, in addition, the kind of help he offered repeatedly seemed useful to whomever Joe addressed. As time passed, Joe took on a kind of good-father role in the group.

Joe helped but did not put himself in a position to be helped. He never volunteered a case of a difficult interaction. It seemed to the group leader that, after only two months of group meetings, Joe had effectively established a position of relative invulnerability in the group. He accomplished this through this opening speech where he warned younger members of the group not to teach him, through the careful and selective content of his occasional contributions in the group, and, certainly, through an occasional frankness about a vulnerability he spoke about but did not act from (when he spoke at the first meeting of the group he could say, "I need help, in particular with conflict . . ."). Joe had staked out a "turf" or, put differently, an image of fatherly wisdom which seemed, to the group leader, to stand in the way of what Joe presumably came to the group to do—learn.

The one challenge to this fatherly stance came from a younger member of the group after Joe revealed, implicitly, on a rare occasion of talking about himself, that in his previous principalship of sixteen years he had been seen as a kind of "father" in the community. The group member, Sam, asked Joe if he hadn't assumed a leadership position in this learning group which mirrored his idea of himself in his first job. And, the younger member asked, curiously, if this were so, wasn't Joe unknowingly making it difficult for himself to get the help he said he needed? Wasn't his father-wise image protecting him, keeping him apart and "safely in control"? Joe was struck by the comparison between how he presented himself in this group and his idea of himself in his first job, but he did not invite discussion. If anything, he discouraged it.

The younger member's questioning of Joe was prompted in part by Joe's describing how for sixteen of his twenty years in the principalship he worked in a lower-middle-class community which was stable and was uniform in attitudes and expectations, particularly about education. Though there were difficult problems, Joe contended with them as a "knight in shining armor." As he said, "I never would have admitted it, but I saw myself this way on occasion. I was Good fighting Evil, and people saw and applauded this idea of me. I was making it possible for their children to make it in this country through getting an education."

Joe left this community for a job in a community of mixed socioeconomic levels. The population was unstable and characterized by pluralistic and conflicting attitudes and expectations about education and educational leaders. In this new setting Joe was not revered. In fact, he often doubted that he had the respect of a solid minority of people in the community and of members of his staff.

So, when Joe, after seven months of quiet, invulnerable participation spoke the words, "I tried it, and it didn't work," and then followed this remark by telling about the incident with Harry, members of the group could have been understandably uncertain about how to respond. To the group leader, the length and intensity of the silence which followed Joe's presentation of the incident with Harry seemed to speak clearly about everyone's ambivalence toward Joe. That ambivalence was not focused on whether or not to try to be of help. It seemed and then proved to be more focused around *how* to be of help.

When members of the group finally dared to respond to Joe, they used, for the most part, a set of behaviors meant to be helpful but which proved not to be. Joe sat quietly through their attempts to help him, occasionally nodding, a bit bemused, waiting, speaking noncommitally, "Yes, I see what you mean . . . ," "That could be . . . ," "I hadn't thought of that . . ." He answered direct questions.

When a lull came in group members' efforts to help, the group leader asked Joe if he found their efforts useful.

Joe said, "Yes, and . . ." He paused, addressed the other group members, "I felt you wanted to help me out, and that's very important to me; the fact that you wanted to give support . . ." His voice trailed off, as if he intended to continue but couldn't decide what to say. Then the words came, "Yes, it was useful as a general indication of interest and support. But no. Actually your suggestions weren't much help."

Joe's response created another tense, silent moment for him and for others. His face flushed as he finished speaking. Obviously, he felt exposed. He had given the group members negative feedback about their performance, and this alone was unfamiliar enough to halt the group for a moment, especially because this group's subject matter was, in part, how each group member offered help—particularly when negative information was involved in the exchange.

The group leader assumed that there would be a direct relationship between how group members tried to help each other in this group and how they behaved "helpfully" in their work settings. As a consequence, he had audiotaped several early discussions between members of this group, replayed the tapes for them, and engaged them in identifying the types of "helping behavior" they used. Once they had identified three central types of helping behavior, "buck-up behavior," "advice-giving behavior," and "information-seeking behavior", each group member was asked to say why he had offered help in one of these forms and what he hoped the outcome would be. Having identified the helping behavior and the thinking which led to it, the group members struggled to clarify the assumptions about people and about change which the group leader contended were implicit in their behavior and thinking.

This identical format was used by the group leader to order the group's inquiry into why their attempts to help Joe had failed. Their behavior and thinking about that behavior was:

Buck-up behavior (often called "stroking," "joining-up")

1. "Gee, Joe, the same thing happened to me last year, you remember, I talked about it several months ago . . ." The speaker went on to retell his story, and when questioned about why he offered help as he did, said, "I thought Joe was in bad shape. I thought that by telling my story, you know, he'd at least see that it wasn't just him." When asked about the hoped-for outcome of his attempt to help, this group member said, "I guess I hoped he'd feel better."

2. "These tenured teachers who've been around for year after year, covering their asses . . ." The speaker went on railing about a particular kind of tenured teacher, and when questioned about why he offered help as he did, said, "Hey, he was dealing with one of those idiots, right? And they are evenly distributed through the population. They get to all of us. They're a curse." When asked about the hoped-for outcome of his attempt to help, the group member said, "I hoped . . . well, that he'd see what he was dealing with . . . then he wouldn't take it so hard."

3. "I'll bet you did much better than you think you did, Joe . . . Look at it this way . . ." The speaker went on to give an explanation of how the consequence of Joe's action could be positive, and when questioned about why he offered help as he did, said, "I don't know, I think he was overreacting. He shouldn't have been so discouraged, you know, tomorrow is another day." When asked about the hoped-for outcome of

his attempt to help, the group member said, "I hoped he wouldn't give up."

Advice-giving behavior (often called "correcting" or "straightening out")

4. "Here's how I'd have handled that . . ." The speaker went on to give an alternative way to proceed, and when questioned about why he offered help as he did, said, "To be honest, Joe screwed up. I don't see why he'd have . . ." When asked about the hoped-for outcome of his attempt to help, the group member said, "I hoped to show Joe a better way . . . then he could avoid getting screwed again."

5. "You shouldn't have given the positive feedback before the negative. That was your mistake, I think." When questioned about why he offered help as he did, and what the hoped-for outcome of his attempt to help was, the speaker said, "I hoped, I guess, to keep Joe from repeating the mistake."

6. "Joe, did you think about trying . . . ?" The speaker went on to sketch a different approach. When questioned about why he offered help as he did, the group member said, "I didn't know what to say. I wanted to help him out, but the only thing I could think of didn't sound *too* good and I figured he'd probably thought of it." When asked about the hoped-for outcome of his attempt to help, the speaker said, "I hoped to help him out, you know . . . we're here to help each other."

Seeking-information behavior

7. "What did the Superintendent say to you . . . ?" When questioned about why he offered help as he did, the group member said, "I was wondering why Joe took this teacher on in the first place." When asked about the hoped-for outcome of his attempt to help, the speaker said, "I don't know; maybe that's where the problem is, you see, right in the fact that he shouldn't have done it in the first place."

8. "What happened when he shouted at you, Joe? What did you say?" When questioned about why he offered help as he did and what the hoped-for outcome of his attempt to help would be, the speaker replied, "If I knew what Joe said, then maybe I could think of something else that would work better."

What characterizes the responses within these three categories? Each respondent (1) defines Joe as a problem and (2) takes responsibility for providing a solution to the problem as he defined it.

Generally, Joe is defined as a problem in the sense that he was seen as being *in* something which he should have been *out* of:

JOE AS "IN":

1. "bad shape"
2. error; not seeing Harry correctly

3. "bad spirits"
4. error; "screwed up"
5. "a mistake"

6. trouble of some kind, apparently
7. trouble, because he "shouldn't have done it in the first place"
8. "a mistake," apparently

IF JOE WERE "OUT, HE WOULD:

1. "feel better".
2. see that he was dealing with an "idiot," and apparently be better off for seeing Harry this way.
3. "see that things weren't so bad."
4. "Avoid getting screwed again."
5. be able to "keep . . . from repeating . . . the mistake."
6. be "out" of trouble.
7. be out of trouble, apparently.
8. be able to say something to Harry which would work.

The respondents defined Joe as a problem both in the sense of seeing Joe as *in* something he could be *out* of and in acting to solve Joe's problem by providing solutions or means of getting out of what he was in:

MEANS OF GETTING JOE OUT

1. Tell my story of a similar event
2. Rail about "idiot" teachers
3. Explain how the consequence of Joe's action could be positive
4. Show Joe an alternative
5. Correct Joe's mistake with advice
6. Question Joe, then give alternative
7. Question Joe to test hypothesis about where Joe made his mistake
8. Question to get information to offer a better way of responding to Harry

When the group members focused their attention on the apparent fact that they all defined Joe as *in* something he should be *out* of and acted to solve his problem by getting him out, they discovered two puzzlements: first, that they shared a common approach to helping and, second, that their helping solutions were not helpful to Joe.

They were surprised and puzzled by the apparent similarity of their approach because they had seen themselves as divided into different factions according to their ideas about how to help people change. The two factions were the "Hand Holders" and the "Tough-minded Critics."

The Hand Holders did lots of bucking-up and some information-seeking, arguing that positive reinforcement was the key to growth. They saw their buck-up behavior as support, as positive reinforcement. The result to Joe of being supported would be, generally, that he would "feel better" and "get perspective and see that 'it' wasn't so bad"; the anticipated result of these changes in Joe would be that he wouldn't quit but would keep trying. A key assumption about Joe seemed to be that he lacked the courage to keep trying, or, in short, that he was weak.

Knowledge of this key assumption came to the "Hand Holders" only through concerted questioning by the group leader, who kept asking, "If that happened, then what?" "If indeed that, too, happened, then what?"

The group leader questioned the Tough-minded Critics, too. They tended to use advice-giving and sometimes information-seeking forms of behavior, arguing that you had to tell people what was wrong with their performance and give them an alternative if they were to improve. The result to Joe of knowing where he was wrong and having an alternative would be, generally, that he "would be equipped to change if he wanted to . . . it's up to him now." A key premise seemed to be that Joe lacked not courage but information. If he lacked information and did not find useful what was given him, what did that mean? Maybe he was not weak but stupid, or stubbornly unwilling to learn.

Neither the Hand Holders nor the Tough-minded Critics all agreed that they held these assumptions about Joe as weak or stupid. But, as a whole, they could see that they were responding to a deficiency they saw in Joe of "ability to keep trying" or of information. The group leader related this idea of seeing Joe as deficient to the two common characteristics of defining Joe as *in* something (a deficiency) which he should be *out* of and of acting to rescue or save Joe from that deficiency with a solution.

First, then, the analysis of the group's "helpful behavior" and thinking yielded puzzlement about the similarity between the two factions which were assumed to be different in their approaches to helping. Second, the analyses led to puzzlement about why the "perfectly reasonable" solutions were not found useful by Joe. After all, they were—for the most part—"true" or "right" or "at least real possibilities":

1. The story told about a group member's similar problem was in fact similar.
2. The railing about idiot teachers was correct, in the sense that Harry had been a rigid person, given to protecting himself rather than risking growth.
3. The alternative offered was a decent possibility.
4. The advice given might have been useful in certain situations.
5. Giving negative information first instead of the positive can be a useful approach.
6. The approach offered was a reasonable possibility.

7. Maybe Joe did blow it right at the start.
8. Maybe if Joe had responded differently when Harry shouted, the talk would have gone better.

After being pushed by the group leader to articulate these two puzzlements, the group members were at once annoyed if not angry with the group leader and eager to question Joe about why he had not found their good help useful. Unfortunately, the group had already run past its ending time. After several exchanges about the group members' frustration at not being able to question Joe, it was agreed that the next meeting would begin with this questioning.

Meeting Number Two

After ten minutes of social conversation in Meeting Number Two, the group leader reviewed the uncomfortable conclusion of the last meeting and asked if group members still wanted to question Joe. Several members were eager. Their eagerness disguised a great deal of impatience, anger, and confusion which came out in a tone of, "What's the matter with you, Joe; this kind of help is 'right,' has worked before, should work now." The questioning and commenting on Joe's recalcitrance went on for nearly forty-five minutes.

During that time, Joe stood his ground, uncertain as it was. "I can't tell you *why* I didn't find your help useful to me. I wish I could, but I just don't know." As others continued to push him, the edge of threat sometimes came into his voice. "I do know this. It becomes more and more clear to me that you are concerned for yourselves, more than for me. You aren't asking me about *me*, about what it was like to be on the receiving end of your help. You are telling me why I should have found your help useful, when in fact I told you it was not."

There was an uncomfortable, long silence after Joe's remark. The young man who had challenged Joe's fatherly image, Sam, broke the silence and, when he did, started a set of interactions between Sam, Joe, and Andy which the group leader found very hopeful and exciting.

Sam asked, "Joe, this is the first time you presented a case, right?" Joe agreed, and the younger man continued, "And, are you, say . . . let down, like . . . that we haven't been more helpful to you?"

Joe waited for some time before answering. Then he said, "Yes," firmly. His eyes traveled from man to man in the room communicating threat, apparently daring others to take him on.

The group leader asked Joe if he weren't afraid that others would judge him negatively, as deficient, because of his saying that he was "let down." Joe said that he had not thought in this way, but it made sense to him. He knew for sure that he did not trust the others with the information he'd given them about being "let down."

Joe addressed the young man, Sam, who had asked if Joe were let down, "Still, I'll say thank you."

Genuinely curious, the young man asked, "Why?"

"You spoke to *me*," Joe said, repeating, "to *me*."

The group leader asked, "You felt recognized?"

"Yes," Joe said, then after a moment of reflection, added, "I guess I did . . ."

Another group member, Andy, burst out, "What the hell is *that* supposed to mean, *recognized*?"

There was a short, tense pause. Joe, puzzled, looked directly at Andy but did not speak.

When Andy could not understand what was going on, he often said so in snorts of speech, snarly in tone. His anger would abate quickly as he caught on. In fact, he was often more anxious than angry.

Still angry, Andy said to Joe, "That's insulting, what he [Sam] said to you! You're not going to let this get you down . . . are you?"

"What?" Joe asked, a bit exasperated.

When Andy spoke a third time, his anger had lost its edge; he was still urgent but more unsure, "All I'm saying is, Joe, you're not giving up, are you?"

"Giving up?" Joe said, incredulously. "Who said anything about giving up?"

The brief silence which followed Joe's remark seemed unproductive to the group leader. The two men appeared trapped. The group leader spoke to Andy, "Andy, when you heard the phrase 'let down,' it meant 'quit' to you, right?"

The leader paused, and Andy tentatively nodded yes. The leader continued, "When Sam said to Joe that Joe might be 'let down' and Joe agreed, you—did that make you think Joe was making himself look small?"

"Yeah, that's right," Andy proclaimed.

Joe said to Andy, "Look, so I was let down. To me, that's not reason to quit trying to figure out how to work with Harry, or, for that matter, reason to quit the group, if that's what you're thinking."

"Good," Andy said, "It's good that you're not thinking of leaving . . . I guess that's what I was worried about."

As he had done in the past, the group leader said that he would like to stop the action of dialogue and review two interactions which had just occurred: first, the interaction between Andy and Joe and, second, the one between Sam and Joe which preceded and precipitated the Andy/Joe exchange.

"I thought that the talk between Andy and Joe during the last few minutes exposed a central fact of human interaction. That fact is that two (or more) people witnessing the same event—here that event was the phrase 'let down'—see and think and feel differently about that event. At first this can seem so simple as to belabor the obvious. But the apparent simplicity and obviousness gives way in the face of the specifics of what just seemed to happen.

"When Sam asked Joe if he were 'let down' and Joe confirmed it, Joe felt that he, Joe, had been 'recognized.' Joe felt gratitude toward Sam.

"On the contrary, Sam's action led Andy to be angered. And, to Andy, the phrase 'let down' meant that Joe might quit the group rather than feel 'recognized.' The phrase which left Joe feeling good left Andy feeling troubled.

"How do we explain this? One way is to imagine that each of us, in this situation, Joe and Andy, brings to a particular event a set of screens or lenses through which we view the event. These screens or lenses might be likened to slices from a large chunk of Swiss cheese.* In effect, we each view the world through the holes of our own slice of Swiss cheese. Andy looks out through the holes in his slice at the phrase 'let down,' and he gets troubled, thinks Joe is saying he'll quit the group, and feels that Joe is demeaning himself by admitting to be 'let down.' Joe, on the other hand, hears Sam ask him if he, Joe, feels 'let down,' and looking through his Swiss cheese, Joe appreciates what Sam asked him and feels 'recognized.'

"In short, as I have tried to say in earlier meetings, but without the benefit of the example provided by Andy and Joe, this course rests on the premise that each of us makes our own meaning of events through the use of screens or lenses. Meaning does not lie in events themselves but is created within. Our resourcefulness as learners and leaders in helping others learn is measured in part by the repertoire of lenses we can bring to view and try to make sense of an event.

"At the risk of unfairly using Andy as a guinea pig, I want to illustrate concretely the concept of lens/screen/filter. You find me using the word *assumption* synonymously with these words. An assumption which Andy seemed to make might be stated this way: if a person feels let down, he or she is bound to give up, to quit. Following from this assumption are Andy's thoughts and feelings: he thought of Sam as insulting, he thought of Joe as quitting, he felt 'worried' and perhaps afraid that Joe would leave. Following from these thoughts and feelings were Andy's actions: he tried to rescue Joe, to keep him from 'giving up' and possibly quitting the group.

"To reverse the order of this cause-and-effect sequence, actions follow

*Kiyo Morimoto, unpublished manuscript, *The Context for Learning.*

from thoughts and feelings, which follow from our assumptions (or lenses, Swiss cheese). It is because our assumptions shape our thoughts, feelings, and actions that I think it is crucial for us to discover them, to test them for validity, and to alter them if the information we get through testing indicates that they are too limited to explain the information adequately.

"For example, the information Andy got from Joe seemed to me to call into question the assumption I attributed to Andy. Joe said that allowing himself to feel 'let down' did not mean he was giving up or quitting. He felt better not worse as a result of Sam's recognizing his feeling of disappointment. On the basis of this information, an alternative to Andy's assumption might be: If a person can fully feel let down when he is let down (rather than maintain that he isn't), then he might feel better about himself.

"This alternative assumption seems to me to allow more latitude for action than the one I said Andy might hold. Andy's assumption seems to confine him to protecting or to rescuing as his only courses of action. That is, he aims at protecting Joe from feeling 'let down' in the first place or if this cannot be done, at rescuing Joe from the disappointment he is *in*.

"In contrast, the alternative assumption would allow for protection and rescue as courses of action *and* for other courses of action as well.

"I can illustrate this idea of an expanded repertoire of action based on an expanded repertoire of assumptions by commenting on the interaction between Sam and Joe. Sam did not try to rescue Joe, to keep Joe from feeling 'let down.' Sam said to Joe, 'And, are you, say . . . let down, like . . . that we haven't been more helpful to you?' Such a response would not be possible within the limits of the assumption I attributed to Andy. That assumption said, 'If a person feels let down, he or she is bound to give up, to quit.' To take Sam's action within the limits of Andy's assumption would be impossible because to do so would be equivalent to inviting the other person, Joe, to give up, quit."

As the group leader paused before trying to say why he had gone into these ideas at such length and depth, Andy said to the group, referring to the leader, "Look at him, he's in a trance again." Andy was smiling. He continued to poke fun at the leader directly, "Listen, how many times do we have to tell you, you're talking to administrators, not Ph.D. candidates."

"Yes," Brian interjected, "speak to us dummies as dummies." Brian seldom spoke without sarcasm. He took a cynical stance about most everything. In particular, he liked to put Andy on.

Andy's comments about and to the group leader were part of a running joke which focused sometimes on the leader's weakness for "fancy thinking" and at other times on the group members' assumptions about themselves as men in action roles who had no time for the luxury of thought.

"Did you finish your shtick?" Brian asked the leader, much to the leader's surprise. Brian seldom made an opportunity for someone else to speak; usually he was busy pronouncing.

"No, and I'd like to, thanks," the group leader said to Brian.

"Yeah, but get to the point," Andy cracked.

"You miss the train?" the leader asked Andy.

"Miss the train? I was traveling by boat, and it went under ten minutes ago," Andy quipped, and got a laugh from everyone.

"To hell with your boat; is your head still above the water," the leader asked.

"I'm sucking water," Andy laughed.

This exchange led into fifteen minutes of discussion about "what the hell you [the leader]" were talking about, as Andy put it delicately. At first, Andy's willingness to talk about his confusion led to further exploration of the ideas presented by the group leader. But soon the force of Andy's search, combined with questions from another group member, Ray, led back to Joe.

"Joe," Andy asked, beseechingly, "Tell me the truth. You're not putting us on, are you?"

"No, no . . ." Joe said, frustrated. "I don't know what I'd be 'putting on' about."

"Look," Andy said urgently, "you got a lot of smart guys here." Andy motioned around the group, beginning to speak haltingly, "Maybe not so experienced as you . . . but . . . we're not dummies; at first you say we didn't help, then you're 'let down,' besides." Andy was struggling visibly to articulate what he couldn't make sense of. "I mean, we gave you the best we had . . ."

The leader spoke into an uncomfortable pause, addressing Andy but speaking generally, "I was talking before about lenses or assumptions, and an assumption which comes to mind as you speak, Andy, is: If something is wrong and I can't right it, then something must be wrong with it (in this instance, Joe) or me (in this instance, you, Andy). Might this be a lens you're viewing this situation from?"

Andy stared, thinking.

Brian said, "Look who's in the trance now."

Andy paid no attention. "Hell, say that again." The leader repeated. Andy said, "Yeah, so what?" with a hint of suspicion.

"It could account for your difficulty in making sense of Joe's actions in our last meeting and today," the leader said tentatively.

"How's that?" Andy asked, still cautious.

"I think you admire Joe, right? There's nothing wrong with him, so to speak. And you've also got information that all the rest of you, you included, Andy, can't be 'wrong'—so the information won't fit the assumption. If you think of assumptions like cookie cutters you're putting down on the dough of your experience with Joe and the group, then the one you're using won't contain the dough."

"Butcher, *baker*, and candlestick maker," Andy exclaimed. "Where does that leave me?"

"Well," the leader offered, "what if you looked at what's happened with Joe from a different lens or assumption: If something is wrong, and I can't right it, then maybe I need more information."

Andy interrupted, upset. "That's just what I was trying to do before you started talking about assumptions again!"

"Yes, but maybe you were looking in the wrong place," the leader needled Andy.

"You're getting to be a regular mystic," Andy said, smiling, but annoyed.

"Okay, here's more black magic for you," the leader said. "What if you had asked yourself this question before addressing Joe minutes ago—'I wonder what was going on inside Joe as we tried to give him help, and it didn't work? What might he have been thinking and feeling? Maybe if I had some information of that kind, I could make more sense of why my help wasn't useful.'"

"I get it," Ray interjected. He had not spoken since the first forty-five minutes when the group members questioned Joe.

"Get what?" Andy asked, a little defensive.

"That's what Sam did," Ray said. "He thought about what was going on inside Joe, with that stuff about 'let down.'"

"What are you saying?" Andy burst out at the leader, "that we're 'spozed to probe each other's private business? I'll tell you, that's not my upbringing. That's nosy. MYOB, that's my way of thinking!"

Sam was upset. "So your way of thinking makes me a jerk."

Referring to Andy, Brian said, "He wouldn't put it just that way, but if you insist . . ."

"Brian, you're trivial," Andy snapped to everyone's surprise; *trivial* was one of Brian's favorite words. "Sam," Andy said, "I like you, but I thought you were nosing where you didn't belong."

"I'm not defending Sam," Joe said deliberately and stopped. "Maybe I am. Anyway, I didn't see what Sam did as invading my privacy. He asked me a very tentative question, and I—"

Andy interrupted. "See, Joe, if somebody else was telling me that he felt good admitting he was let down, I wouldn't believe him! But *you* saying it, hearing it from you . . ."

"I've got to go," Ray said. "It's late." It was late, and the group reluctantly began to break up. This was an awkward end because Andy was still "up in the air," as one group member put it.

Andy tried for the last word. "So, you're all going to leave me here sucking water, right?" He was smiling, but obviously pained.

"Men do not live by guilt alone," Brian jabbed at Andy. "You will, unfortunately, outlive us all."

Andy was shaking his head. "I wonder what that guy is all about, sometimes."

"You might ask him," the leader needled Andy, and then stayed to talk with Andy alone.

Meeting Number Three

The group leader began Meeting Number Three by reviewing Meeting Number One.

"At the meeting before our last one, we analyzed the helping behavior you used with Joe in an effort to get to guiding assumptions. I pushed you quite hard, and I know that some, perhaps all of you, did not agree that the Hand Holders were guided in thought and action by an assumption that Joe was weak. Likewise, it seemed to me that the Tough-minded Critics were guided by the assumption that Joe was dumb, lacking in information, and 'stubborn' for not accepting good information from you.

"It did seem to all of us that both factions were bound together by the fact that each defined Joe as *in* a deficiency which they took responsibility for getting him *out* of through offering different kinds of solutions meant to rescue him.

"Today, I want you to listen to the audiotape and read a transcript of Joe's presentation of Harry not from the perspective that Joe is *in* a deficiency but, if possible, first from the perspective that Joe is *in* an attempt to make sense of his experience and, second, from the perspective that you don't have to get him *out* of what he is *in.* You don't have to rescue him.

"Necessarily, this request will tax your trust in me again. It might not make sense right now or later. Rather than discussing it in the abstract, though, please listen to the tape and read the transcript."

Once again, Joe's story was:

I knew before we started talking that I would have to tell Harry some negative things about his teaching and that he wouldn't like it, but I just couldn't wait any longer. The parents are on my back, and I'm having a terrible time just finding enough kids to fill his class next year.

In addition, the Superintendent is hearing from some school committee members, and I am hearing from him.

Harry came into my office with that blank look on his face, and I started off trying to make him feel at ease. I got some coffee, and we made some nervous comments about the weather. I talked positively about an assembly that he had recently organized.

Then, I began to drop the other shoe and tell him about the parents who are sending me notes and phoning me about him. He sits there with that stony look, and when I stop talking, he says, "Why haven't you told me this before!"—almost a shout.

From here on it all goes downhill—polite, after the outburst, but no one is listening to me, and I'm not hearing him. Then it's over, and he leaves, and I say to myself, "Well, what's the use?"

After playing the tape of this story twice, the group leader asked members of the group to write down what, from the perspective of Joe's being *in* an attempt to make sense of his experience, each of them heard him saying.

All but two members of the group could hear Joe saying that: one, he was discouraged, two, he saw himself as having failed, and, three, he seemed stopped, stuck, trapped.

While these three "readings," as Joe called them, were nudged out of the varying responses to Joe's story, Joe got increasingly excited. He became animated, nodding his head, smiling, obviously tickled. The boyishness he allowed was new, charming, and unsettling for some group members.

"What the hell's into you, Joe?" asked Andy, who had gotten angry with Joe at the end of the previous session.

"The devil, I'm afraid," Joe teased. He continued, "This will be hard for you to believe but—I *was* discouraged; I did see myself as failing; I was trapped. But I did *not* know these things at the time! I know them only now that I hear them from you."

This statement created a great deal of commotion in the group, lots of people talking at once.

The group leader tried to focus the various debates by asking Joe what might have happened if, after he had told his story, someone had said, "Joe, you seem pretty discouraged . . ."

Joe said, "I'm not *sure*, of course, but I think I would have said, 'I certainly am . . .'" He paused before continuing, and spoke halfheartedly after a long sigh. "'I really screwed it up.'"

There were several seconds of silence before the group leader replied to Joe.

Flatly, without negative judgment, the leader said, "You were a flop."

Joe's head had been hanging slightly. With the leader's comment, Joe's head jerked up and his mouth opened, seemingly in an attempt to speak before words came. When they did, Joe said, "That's right . . ." and then, with greater conviction, "That's right! I was a flop." He paused, and continued, "I thought I'd do much better . . ."

The leader's "outrageous" comment, "You were a flop," startled several in the group, and Andy, who sometimes served inadvertently as their collective mouthpiece, objected.

Speaking to the group leader, he said, "Hey, what are you doing?"

The leader appealed to Andy, making reference to Joe, "Give him a few minutes." Andy looked puzzled but gradually sat back from the table in deference to the leader's request.

The leader did not want to explain himself at this point because he would be calling attention to what he did rather than keeping the focus on Joe.

The leader saw his comment, "You were a flop," as similar to his earlier question to Joe, "Joe, you seem pretty discouraged?" Both were attempts to "acknowledge" the experience and sense Joe seemed to be making of his efforts with Harry. The leader hoped that if he could demonstrate that he heard the sense Joe was making and show that he thought it legitimate, then Joe might, too.

The leader's response followed from his sense that Joe was caught in limbo between feeling discouraged, on the one hand, and, on the other, thinking he shouldn't be; between seeing himself as a failure and thinking he shouldn't see himself this way. In effect, the leader imagined Joe trapped between contending parts of himself, his feelings and his judgments about them; and hence immobilized.

The effect of legitimizing Joe's right to feel discouraged and a failure was paradoxical: a full immersion into, or, to put it differently, assertion of his own sense ("I certainly am . . . [discouraged]". "That's right! I was a flop") would hopefully result in distance and the opportunity for choice and recommitment to try to make new sense of the painful dilemma he found himself in.

When Joe began to speak again, his tone was reflective, and he provided new information about what happened with Harry. Where his first presentation supplied, for the most part, a picture of external events, this second presentation provided information about his internal events as he tried to talk with Harry.

You know, you remember how I told you he came in with that blank look on his face? Well, at that moment something froze inside me, and a little voice said, "Well, you're not going to get anywhere with this one. It's hopeless."

But I kept trying. . . .

I kept trying to think of all the things I know or think I know about evaluation and supervision. I've been to enough workshops over the years.

But nothing came back, nothing helped. . . .

I just couldn't focus . . . my head was swimming with . . . just swimming.

"So, in a way, you were kind of overwhelmed . . .?" the group leader asked Joe.

Joe said, sadly, "Yes . . . I guess I was, was—I couldn't gather myself, somehow . . ."

"Well, you were feeling that your efforts were doomed from the outset, I take it?" the leader asked.

"From the second I saw his stony face, I think. . . ."

"Do you have any notion what there was about that stony face that—"

Joe cut in, "It was," he began to speak haltingly, "was cold . . . hard . . ."

There were several seconds of silence.

"Maybe," the group leader said tentatively, "maybe you were pretty frightened . . . and yet felt you shouldn't be . . .?"

Joe hesitated before answering, "Afraid?" He paused again before beginning to laugh, "I think I was scared shitless." He made this statement with little ambivalence and no apology. From the group leader's perspective Joe was acknowledging the fear, thereby making it a resource rather than allowing it to remain a liability. It would have remained a liability as long as Joe was unknowingly caught between partly feeling it and partly thinking he shouldn't.

Joe continued laughing, "You know, for four years I've tiptoed around Harry as if he were a time bomb set to go off with a touch of negative comment. When I first came, the stories I heard about Harry—I think I was put on the defensive, you know, at a time when I had so much else to think about. Then, I forgot about my initial fear. I guess it went underground. My thoughts were on what a 'trial' Harry was."

"Maybe, in a way," suggested the group leader, "you figured that if you could be that scared, how could you possibly be a leader?"

"Listen," Joe exclaimed, excited, "I was no more afraid then than I am now . . . What did you say?"

The group leader was afraid, too, smiling nervously, wondering if he'd pushed Joe too far. The leader had hoped to test, by imagining out loud, the assumption which might underly Joe's reluctance to claim his fear as a resource.

The leader said to Joe, "I think you heard what I said."

"I did," Joe responded, "but it makes me nervous." He paused, "So you're saying that leaders can't be afraid and still lead?"

"No," the group leader responded, "I'm asking whether maybe, in a part of you, you make that assumption: if afraid, then weak and unfit for leadership—in short, a fraud."

Joe was at once startled and beginning to break up in laughter. He laughed uncontrollably for a while, much to the discomfort of several other members of the group. Joe's laughter was clumsily punctuated by unsuccessful attempts to say, "A fraud . . . a fraud, I always thought I was a fraud." Joe's laughter stopped the group for several minutes.

The assumption, framed by the group leader as, "If afraid, then weak and unfit for leadership—in short, a fraud" was, of course, absurd. It can't be held, rationally. If, in the course of an ordinary discussion about leadership,

Joe were asked if he held this assumption, he would in all likelihood have said, "No, of course not."

But this was no ordinary discussion, obviously, and Joe's uncontrolled laughter indicated to the group leader that Joe was encountering an assumption about the relationship between parts of himself, held at an emotional rather than intellectual level. The group leader believed that assumptions about oneself held at an emotional level guided the day-to-day behavior of leaders and had to be encountered and claimed as "that's where I'm really at" if behavior were to be changed consciously, by choice, and through commitment to more positive assumptions about self and role.

As Joe's laughter subsided, he said to the others, "Bear with me, bear with me, I'm okay. In fact, I haven't felt so good in, in . . ." His voice trailed off. Two group members got up to get coffee.

Apparently quite moved by what had been happening for Joe, Sam, Joe's young friend, spoke, "You remember, Joe, several months ago I thought you were really protecting yourself with that father-wise image of yours—"

Sam was looking at Joe and asking a question which Joe answered, "I certainly do, and what you said preyed on my mind heavily for those two months. It nudged me to join the hordes of mortal men." Joe smiled, affectionately.

Sam continued, somewhat caught off guard, apparently by Joe's acknowledgment of how Sam had been of help, "Well, somehow, I don't know, I just didn't think *you* would have all of these, these . . . you were . . . that scared when you were with Harry?" Sam was staggering from word to phrase to word.

Joe gave him time to continue, and when Sam did not, Joe said, "Do you wish that I weren't so, what?—frightenable?"

Sam answered, "Yes, I guess I do . . ."

"Disappointing, eh?" the group leader said.

"You know it," Sam replied, "I mean, I knew it in my head, you know; leaders are people and people are often afraid, but seeing Joe, well, I guess I figure there's a point of arrival out there, you know, where, well, you've got it all together."

Andy spoke to Joe and Sam. "No offense, but it's getting late," and then, turning to the group leader, continued, "I'll tell you, I'm having a hard time fitting this today and last time with why we're here. We're here to get better at helping people change, right? Well, what's all this got to do with that?"

"What's 'all this'?" Joe asked, a little defensively.

"No offense, Joe," Andy said. "I guess this has been good for you, but I'm still not sure what's going on . . ."

"I'll give it a try," the group leader said, deciding to take Andy's request literally. "I think our own ability to grow and help someone else grow depends directly on how capable we are of imagining how another person might be experiencing internally the observable events he's involved in. So, for example, during our last meeting I thought that Sam was able to imagine out loud what Joe's experience of not getting help was like *for Joe*—a 'let down.' A prerequisite to our extending our imagination to others, as Sam did to Joe, is our finding and claiming parts of ourselves which through the years we have lost touch with; parts of ourselves which we have declared "off limits" or "illegitimate"; parts of ourselves who are strangers to us if not dangerous aliens. To the extent we can reclaim these parts of ourselves as friends rather than banishing them as enemies, we become capable of imagining how other people experience events differently from us. We thereby take a crucial step toward enhancing our ability to foster growth, theirs and ours.

"My theory of how we 'lose' parts of ourselves which we must 'find' and welcome back goes like this. At an early time in our lives, we learn through our parents and through other people of importance to us that certain feelings, thoughts, and actions are 'off limits.' Out of the necessity of surviving in the settings of our early life, upon which we are entirely dependent, we try to banish those 'parts' of ourselves which others do not accept. But we can't rid ourselves of them entirely. As a consequence, we are in conflict between the fact that they exist and the accompanying meanings which say they should not exist.

"Joe seemed to be in conflict between feeling afraid and thinking he shouldn't be. As he recognized this conflict, he was able to break it and reclaim his fear as a legitimate part of himself. His asserting his right to his fear puts him in control of it rather than having it control him. It makes the fear a part of a larger whole self rather than allowing it to diminish the whole. It makes the fear a potential resource rather than a liability.

"What I've called a *conflict* between feeling and the thought that condemns the feeling can also be talked about in terms I've used before—as a lens or an assumption. For example, continuing with Joe, Joe's assumption might be, If afraid, then weak and unfit for leadership. If Joe holds this assumption, it will keep him from feeling afraid even if he is.

"Here are a set of assumptions which many leaders tend to hold about themselves:

If I am fearful,	then I am a coward or weakling.
If I am sad,	then I am a sissy, weak.
If I am angry	then I am either all-mighty or out of control.
If I am uncertain,	then I am wishy-washy, weak.
If I don't know,	then I am stupid.
If I am unable to make sense,	then I am dumb, stupid.
In general, if I have these feelings,	then I am unfit for leadership.

"Unfortunately, the result of these assumptions seems to be that the leader who holds them is unfit for *learning*. His intellect is tied up in fending off the alien parts of himself in the left-hand column, and consequently it is not available imaginatively to enter the inner world of another person distinct in character from himself. It is this imaginative leap expressed through empathy which nurtures growth in the other person as well as in oneself."

Andy said, "I like the sound. I like the passion. But I'm not sure I get the drift."

"Still sucking water?" Brian jabbed.

"What would you know about it?" Andy said. "You're too chicken to get involved in anything but sniping."

Their exchange, as usual, was sharp but not bitter. The ending time for the group had come. Several members left. Others stayed and talked informally, mixing an occasional question about the group leader's closing presentation with general conversation.

Meeting Number Four

The group leader began Meeting Number Four by explaining his intent for the day. He wanted the group members to shift their attention from helping Joe make new sense of what had happened with Harry to helping Joe invent new forms of action which Joe might use in future encounters with Harry. What new assumptions and behaviors might allow Joe the hope of not repeating his past negative performance?

Andy cut in, "Listen, no offense, Joe." Andy faced the group leader. "Joe's been getting plenty of time here recently. And I don't want to screw up your plan today, but, you remember a couple of times ago I tried to get into the act here . . . you know what I mean," Andy looked around to others. "Now, I don't want to screw things up, you know?" Though Andy had always been an active participant, he had never asked explicitly for time for himself before. As a consequence, the group leader was torn; he wanted to invite Andy to continue but also wanted to focus this meeting on inventing new behavior.

George, generally a silent participant, said, "Andy, I heard you've got the pressure on you."

"Yes," Andy said. "The Superintendent gave me the word again about a couple of my people, and so I gave one of them the word, you know—and, something funny happened."

The group leader addressed the whole group, explaining his ambivalence and then suggesting the group might work both with Andy's concerns and the idea of inventing new behavior.

The leader proposed, "Three sessions ago we engaged in a rigorous analysis of how you attempted to help Joe when he presented his case. That analysis, hopefully, brought a new perspective and, possibly, some clarity to your thinking about how you tend to offer help. Instead of using Joe as the guinea pig today, I'll ask you all to be guinea pigs. I want each of you to try to help Andy, but attempt to alter your behavior according to the results of the analysis three sessions ago. In short, don't look at Andy as a problem you have to solve; in other words, don't try to get him *out* of what he's *in*; don't buck-up, give advice, or ask for specific bits of information.

"Obviously, you will feel muzzled and handicapped, perhaps unfairly. In asking you to take on this task, I am not saying that buck-up, advice-giving, and information-seeking behaviors are useless or bad; I am not saying that you consciously attempt to define others as weak or stupid, hence deficient. I realize, too, that some of you didn't buy the results of our analysis—you don't believe you defined Joe as deficient in the first place."

There were several nods of agreement from group members.

The leader continued, "I've said what *not* to do, if possible. What *can* you do? I'm asking you to take what you've learned about offering help and translate those learnings into new forms of helping." The key idea here is translating and this involves inventing new behaviors based on new assumptions.

"You might use the following guidelines to aid you in inventing:

"Ask Andy what happened, both observably and inside him as the observable acts occurred.

"Assume that Andy will be *in* not a deficiency but a search, a process characterized by words like "seeking," "pursuing," "puzzling," "groping," "floundering," or, if his search is stalled, words like "stewing," "worrying," "troubling"; try to let Andy know what you hear him saying about the process rather than get him *out* of it.

"When you sense that Andy is stuck or trapped, ask yourself what might the information Andy has shared about his acts, thoughts, and feelings mean *to him*?"

There was an uncomfortable silence when the leader stopped speaking.

Brian said, sarcastically, "You don't ask much, do you?"

"You're right, I do," the leader said. "I've never asked a group to work on translating in this open-ended way before, focusing attention on a member of the group. It might not work. It will be difficult, uncomfortable, and self-conscious."

The leader paused and spoke directly to Andy. "Perhaps most of all for you, Andy. If we're too awkward and the interaction is cumbersome, we'll stop and try something else."

There followed several minutes of discussion about the task. The discussion ended when George spoke for the second and last time. Timidly, he asked Andy, "What happened that was 'funny'?"

Andy seemed to hear George but was watching Joe. "No offense, Joe? You know, I feel bad taking the time away. I can use it, though. . . ." Andy's head and upper body were nodding from side to side, like a metronome. Joe had indicated several times with a turn of his head that he took "no offense." Still speaking to Joe, Andy said, "I think I saw you take the leap, you know, and I said to myself, 'Hey, why not, maybe I'll get something out of it.' Right? You're there anyway, so why not?"

Joe was right there, anyway, saying, "What did happen?"

Andy began to tell a story in a disjointed way, speaking fast, in an increasingly exclamatory manner:

"Look," I said to this assistant principal of mine. "You've gotta stop being so tough on these teachers." We've been through this, you know, years ago.

I don't know what it is with this guy. Nice guy, you know. I get on with him fine.

But the Superintendent, he's on my back, says he's hearing from school committee about my assistant.

Christ, what people will tell other people; nothing's sacred anymore.

So, all I said was, "Just back off a bit," you know, and this assistant of mine goes through the roof. I didn't even say anything, you know?

Andy paused for a moment and another group member who had spoken only a few times as yet, Ray, filled the gap. Ray was trying to be considerate but his impatience mixed the message he sent, "Andy, I can't follow you. You're skipping all around. Can't you slow down?"

"Yeah, okay, okay," Andy said. "But, what do you think, I didn't even say anything to this guy and he blows his stack, right there in front of me, just like the Superintendent said he does with teachers; he really mouths 'em down."

"He what?" Ray asked, more impatient than before. Andy had not slowed down at all. If anything, he talked faster after the last time Ray spoke.

Andy answered Ray, like a man trying to brush away an irritating fly, "He gives 'em lip, puts 'em down—mouths 'em down."

The group leader was aware of the effort which Ray was putting into helping Andy, but Ray was getting in the way, badly. His remarks were, from the leader's perspective, irrelevant to Andy's attempt to share and make sense. Ray's questions seemed generated from his needs, his feelings of impatience and confusion, and perhaps loss of control at not being able to follow Andy's story. He seemed to assume that to be of help he had to grasp an orderly flow of the literal account of what Andy said. Since Andy was not speaking in an orderly way or literally, Ray had, as a result of his assumption about giving help, taken on himself the task of getting Andy "straightened out" before Ray could be of help. In short, Ray had defined Andy as *in* a deficiency which he, Ray, had to get Andy *out* of.

It seemed to the group leader that Andy was saying, and wanted to have heard, that he was anxious and afraid. He wanted to be able to make sense of what had happened between him and his assistant but he could not, so he was trapped.

Ray appeared ready to speak again, and though Andy seemed irritated with Ray's questions, Andy was watching Ray.

Joe muscled in by calling Andy's name, "Andy, I thought that what bothered you was when the Assistant 'blew his top'?"

"Yeah, yeah, Andy said immediately, physically moving toward Joe. "What'd you think of that, Joe? What'd you make of that?"

The group leader liked Joe's response to Andy for two reasons. It recognized Andy as concerned rather than as deficient and acknowledged the existence of Andy's attempt to search for meaning ("bothering") and in that way nurtured the effort. The leader's bias was, obviously, toward nurturing the part of Andy who sought his own "sense," as opposed to the part of him who would have others tell him what sense he should make, thereby rescuing him in the short run but leaving him dependent on others to make sense for him over the long run.

The second reason the group leader liked Joe's response to Andy was its focus on the part of the interaction between Andy and his assistant (when the Assistant "blew his top") which Andy had already mentioned twice. The fact that Andy repeated this incident twice indicated its importance to him and gave direction to where the "helpers" might focus their attempts to be helpful, if they could avoid Andy's invitation and their natural tendency to define him as deficient and rescue him from his own frustrating attempts to make new sense.

When Andy had asked Joe, "What'd you think of that, Joe? What'd you make of that?" Joe turned up his hands, and said, "I don't know . . ." He appeared to be searching for another response but his hesitation left a silence which Ray filled. Ray's patience had gone.

"You should have set your assistant straight," Ray told Andy. "He's got no right to blow up at you. You were trying to help him out. Who does he think he is?" Though well meaning, Ray's response was unfortunate, when viewed from the group leader's perspective.

Ray had defined Andy as *in* a deficiency, lacking apparently in courage or intelligence to "set straight" his assistant. It seemed that Ray hoped to rescue

Andy by giving Andy information that his assistant was out of line in blowing up at his boss.

At this point Brian chimed in, speaking first to the group leader, flippantly, "I know I'm not supposed to say this," and then, turning to Andy, "but, Andy, wherever you got this assistant, he's defective merchandise and you ought to return him—"

Andy interrupted, "Yes, yes, very funny, but you don't see. I get along with this guy just fine, just fine, a nice guy. I like him, and I . . ." Andy was talking very fast again, and paused, momentarily lost for words.

The group leader addressed the part of Brian's previous comment which had been directed at the leader ("I know I'm not supposed to say this") by asking Brian if Brian weren't frustrated with the assignment which called on group members to try to figure out how to respond to Andy in ways which did not define Andy as deficient.

Brian replied immediately, in the cynical tone which tended to be a regular part of his style, "You're asking us to baby Andy. He's no Little Red Riding Hood. You don't have to protect him from us wolves." Brian looked around the table at other group members, smiling a bit anxiously, apparently trying to gather support for his position.

The leader said to Brian, "I'm not concerned about whether or not Andy can take what you dish out. I'm sure he can. But I am concerned about how nourishing your vittles are: Do they enlarge his opportunity to make new sense, for himself, or do they more centrally serve your need to fill him up quickly and get him away from this table (to push a metaphor much too far)? Brian, I think you want to help Andy, but you seem trapped in the confines of having to define him as deficient in order to be of help. The difficulty with that approach is that, practically speaking, it doesn't work over the long run."

"Terrific," Brian said, caustically, but then expressed his frustration, his sense of loss at how to go about interacting differently, "But, what am I supposed to *do*, sit here and nod knowingly like some damn shrink. I'm an administrator, not a shrink!"

The group leader replied, "It can feel as if the only alternative to toughening Andy up is to be nice to him, to pretend that you understand with fake nods of approval. But I think there's a lot of ground between those extremes. Taken from our work in this group so far, here is another cut at guidelines you might use to seek a different stance toward helping Andy:

"Find out what was said between Andy and his assistant.

"As Andy tells what was said, listen for cues which indicate the particular points in the exchange which give *Andy* cause for concern.

"Check with Andy to see if he finds himself concerned about those parts in the exchange which you have identified as of concern to him.

"Invite Andy to stop and recount what he was thinking and feeling at a particular point in the exchange which concerns him.

"Try to imagine out loud what assumptions might give rise to these thoughts and feelings."

The group leader had gotten preoccupied with formulating these guidelines and was startled when Joe cut in, "Listen, I think we're letting Andy drift here." He looked at the leader, who said, "You're right," and at Brian, who shrugged his shoulders noncommitally. Turning his head to Andy, Joe asked, "Andy, what did the Assistant say, actually; he must have said something when he blew up?"

Andy lit up, as if Joe had plugged him into an electric socket. "He said I didn't know what I was talking about, that I was listening to a few troublemakers on the staff who didn't have the professional judgment to know when they were wrong. And he didn't like *me* accusing him of unprofessional conduct; it wasn't *all* teachers he had a bad time with."

"Yes, yes," Sam said excitedly. He had not spoken during this meeting. "Andy," he asked, hesitantly, "What was going on inside you as the Assistant said these things?"

Unhesitatingly, Andy said, "I'm saying to myself, what's got into this guy? *I* didn't say he was *unprofessional.* I'm just telling him to back off a bit, you know. You know, Sam, I *like* the guy, I'm not trying to mouth him down. I'm trying to *help* him."

Sam stayed right with Andy by asking, "And what did you say back to your assistant?"

Andy hesitated, moving uncomfortably in his chair. His eyes narrowed, as if in fear. Then his words burst out, "I said, 'What are you, crazy? This is no big deal. Don't take it so hard.' And so on—I don't know, I just didn't know what else to say."

Apparently acting from an interest in continuing to play out the group leader's guidelines, Joe said to Andy, "You didn't like what you said, did you?"

Andy responded, "No."

"What didn't you like?" Joe asked.

"Joe," Andy said, "I count on my assistant. I'd hate like hell to lose him."

Ray, who had lost his patience earlier, jumped in, questioning Andy. "Who said you'd lose him, the Superintendent?" Ray was oblivious to the inappropriateness of his question as judged from the perspective of aiding Andy in his search to make sense. The question called Andy's attention away from his efforts to account for what happened with his assistant and, in effect, asked Andy to attend to Ray's needs to be "filled in."

Andy said, "No," to Ray, trying to ignore the question. Andy's eyes were holding on to Joe.

Looking a bit lost, Joe turned toward the group leader. The leader asked Joe, "You're not sure where to go from there?" and Joe nodded yes.

The leader asked Andy, "How are you doing?"

"No problem," Andy said, pausing before beginning to speak again. "Now, I think what bothers me is, I never actually told my assistant the bad stuff I got from the Super, and . . . to be honest, teachers complain to me, too . . ."

There was a silence of several seconds.

"So," Joe said, tentatively, gathering himself, "maybe you say to yourself, if I really told my assistant all the negative information, I'd lose him for sure . . . If he blew up when I 'did nothing,' then disaster would result—?"

"That's right! That's right!" Andy exclaimed. "Look how he blew up when I went easy, downplayed the whole thing. If I gave him the whole ball of wax . . ." Andy's voice trailed off.

The silence was tense.

Brian spoke. "Look, Andy, I put you on a lot. Put that aside. I don't know, really, what I'm doing here . . ." Brian paused, and while he did, the leader sat in pleasant surprise. For the first time during these group sessions, Brian had begun to make himself vulnerable, to risk the discomfort and self-consciousness of trying out new ideas and behavior.

Brian continued, "But, I'm coming up with the word *trapped,* again. You sound trapped . . ." Brian paused and Andy waited, very still.

"If you go 'easy' on your assistant, you lose; if you go hard, you lose; if you do nothing, you lose . . . is that what's got you trapped . . .? Brian's voice was tentative at the end, asking not attributing.

Andy began nodding yes, sadness filling his face for the first time the leader could remember. It would be difficult for him to accept help from Brian, let alone feel comforted by the help offered. Andy seemed on the verge of feeling comforted, of feeling the release which can come from being "*recognized,*" known for who and where you are in a particular moment in time.

When Andy spoke, he talked first to Brian and then to Joe, looking occasionally at Sam and the leader. His voice was tired, softened, slowed down. He spoke with ease. "The real point is whether or not I want to keep doing my job. I've been at it more than ten years now, and it's lost its kick.

"Here I am, starting all over again. You understand? I can see that I don't know what's going on in here, some of the time. I think it's necessary, you know, getting new skills. I need 'em. But what I wish most is that my assistant would simply get the hint and get his business in order. You follow me?

"I don't know if I really want to put so much of my time into figuring out how to work with him and the thousand other dismal situations. Dismal. Negative. Everybody is angry, or anxious. I don't enjoy going to work anymore." Andy stopped, saddened.

Andy's words precipitated a half hour of discussion, which included several generally silent members, about the nature of the conditions they each worked in, about the quality of their work lives, and, finally, about why they were in this group.

In the leader's mind, Andy's willingness to risk sharing his doubts and questions, his unfulfilled hopes, his disappointments, provided a rare opportunity for him and others to step back not only from the task in this group but from the event-by-event focus of everyday life. The distance allowed for a shift in focus from *what next* and *how to* to *what for* and *why*.

From the leader's perspective, the *what for* and *why* questions had to do with personal choice and commitment. As he listened to Andy from this perspective, he thought Andy might be asking himself questions like, "Why invest myself in learning when I feel hopeless about my job? What's the use? People used to get the hint; why not now? Am I going to try to change my ways after all these years? Is it possible to change really, and if so, where will it get me?"

The leader tested these questions with Andy, and he confirmed them. Then, several of the silent members spoke again, saying, in effect, that this group had been a curiosity to them. They liked the people—but still—as one member stated his ambivalence, "I'm not so sure this is for me."

The ending time for the group came and passed.

Andy said, reflectively, looking at Joe, "There must be some way for me to, you know, do a better job with my assistant . . ." He paused, then said tentatively, "It's worth the try, don't you think, Joe?"

Joe paused and then said hesitantly, "I wish I could say yes, but, I don't know . . . it's your decision . . ."

"I know," Andy replied, smiling.

"Maybe," the group leader began, "if you had more information, it could help you make that decision, Andy. If Joe were willing, the two of you might meet together before our next meeting and try to invent a different approach to talking with your assistant. The two of you could present that approach the next time we meet, and we would analyze it and re-invent. We would see if we could come up with an approach which isn't "a hint" or "a slam," an approach which provides you with a clear alternative to how you proceeded the first time. Then you can choose whether or not to speak again to your assistant about his performance."

Joe and Andy agreed to the leader's suggestion, and the leader tried to close the group by giving each member a writing assignment. He asked the members to write for fifteen minutes before the next meeting about how their attempt to help Andy differed from how they had helped Joe three meetings before. As the leader talked, Andy waited impatiently and then spoke, attempting to hold members' attention before they left.

"Listen," he said with passion, "I appreciate this time. This is all new to me, and I can't say what happened, but, it's good, it's good . . ." He paused, looking at Joe, and spoke in jest, yet seriously, "It's your fault, you know. You got me in this . . ."

Brian began to laugh, and said to Joe, "And Andy can count on you to get him *out*, too! Right?"

"I hope not," Joe said. "Let's call it a day."

10 | Commentary on Joe's Case

The case just presented is extremely complex in terms of ideas, individual growth, and group interaction. It may, therefore, be useful to summarize briefly the events of each of the four group meetings before discussing the case.

Meeting Number One

Joe presents his case of Harry.

Group leader presents analysis of helping behavior, intentions, and assumptions used by group members to help Joe:

Buck-up

Advice-giving

Information-seeking

Group recognizes similarities between Hand Holders and Tough-minded Critics in that both appear to see persons needing help as deficient. This puzzles them.

Joe states that he does not feel helped by group's efforts to be helpful. This puzzles them further.

Meeting Number Two

Group questions Joe about why he did not find useful the help offered by the group.

Sam asks Joe if he felt "let down."

Joe says he did and thanks Sam for "recognizing" his feelings by asking if he felt "let down."

Andy gets angry and says Sam insulted Joe by his question.

Stop-the-action analysis of Andy-Joe exchange and Sam-Joe exchange reveals different assumptions, giving rise to totally different meanings to phrase "let down."

Group leader discusses assumptions and their centrality in influencing behavior.

Group leader suggests that imagining Joe's inner workings would help to understand why group's help was not effective.

Andy protests that imagining how the other person feels intrudes on a person's privacy. However, he is obviously puzzled at meeting's end.

Meeting Number Three

Group leader reviews Meeting Number One regarding helping behavior and assumptions.

Group undertakes exercise: presentation of tape (twice) of the case of Joe's interaction with Harry, and group writes down what they heard from perspective of Joe's sense making.

Group leader replays response to Joe, this time by legitimizing his discouragement.

This response evokes from Joe new information about Harry, particularly in terms of how Joe felt interacting with Harry.

Joe confronts at an emotional level his assumptions about leaders and fear; he laughs uncontrollably at the idea that he is a fraud as a leader because he is afraid.

Sam acknowledges his hope that being grown up means being finished, complete, perfect.

Andy questions: "What's all this got to do with helping people?"

Group leader discusses growth in terms of claiming conflicted parts of the self and extending imagination to others.

Meeting Number Four

Group leader discusses plan to have group help Joe invent new behaviors.

Andy interrupts, asking for time for himself.

Group leader asks group to try to listen to Andy's case and to help him from the new perspectives of attending to and inquiring into his sense-making.

Andy presents his case of the blow-up with his assistant principal.

Ray interrupts, asking Andy to slow down and make it logical.

Joe attempts to help Andy in a different way by focusing on what "bothered" Andy.

Brian expresses his discomfort: "I'm an administrator, not a shrink."

Group leader formulates another set of guidelines for helping Andy.

Joe interrupts to bring discussion back to Andy by asking Andy to state specifically what the Assistant Principal said.

Sam appears to get the idea of helping by inquiring and being concrete. He asks, "What was going on inside you as the Assistant said those things? . . . And what did you say back . . .?"

Joe says to Andy, "You didn't like what you said, did you?" thereby acknowledging Andy's discomfort.

Joe, then, after having his own confusion acknowledged by the group leader, is able to summarize tentatively one of Andy's assumptions regarding the disastrous results of sharing all the negative information with his assistant.

Brian, for the first time, intervenes unsarcastically and tentatively identifies Andy as trapped.

These responses appear to release Andy, to make him feel recognized in ways Joe claimed the group's earlier responses had not done for him.

When Andy next speaks, he allows himself to be "let down" and to question his commitment to his job and to learning.

Andy then tentatively recommits himself to developing, with Joe's help, some alternative ways of working with the Assistant Principal, which the two of them agree to present to the group at the following meeting.

These are the events of the case. Now we will view those events from the perspective of two of the learning categories: Making New Sense and Translating.

Joe and the Group Make New Sense

The case we have just reviewed is about offering help to people in a way that assumes (1) they make sense of their problem in their own way and that way differs from the way the helper makes sense, (2) they need to stay in their own sense-making efforts in order to grow in their own capacity and confidence, and (3) they should not be "rescued" by a helper's interpretations or violated by a helper's own needs to be in control or be helpful.

A prior condition to offering help in this manner (or even of seeing this sort of help as desirable or effective) is to come to an emotional comprehension of that proposition which most people believe they accept and act from—that people are not the same, that they see the world differently, and that truth is relative. To know this in one's intellect is far different from demonstrating this knowledge in one's actions. Frequently, people act as if at an emotional level they believe others see a situation in the identical way they do.

Clearly, this is true for Andy in his response to Sam's question about feeling let down. Even in the face of evidence from Joe that he appreciated the question, Andy can only perceive the question as insulting and cannot believe that Joe finds it helpful. Andy has no way of understanding what has just gone on in front of him except in terms of his own thought. Andy's assumptions appear to dictate the following rules: a leader should not admit that he feels let down; if he breaks that rule and admits his disappointment, there can be only one outcome: the leader will be overwhelmed by his feelings and will give up.

A measure of Andy's growth throughout the four meetings can be found in the fact that by the end of the final meeting, he allows himself to do exactly what scared him so thoroughly when Joe did it. Andy breaks his internal rules, feels "let down," and contemplates "quitting." What results paradoxically from this experience is renewed commitment to try again. This experience for Andy parallels the experience for Joe which, at the time, Andy found incomprehensible.

To offer help to others from the perspective of imagining their reactions and recognizing them rather than seeing their problems and rescuing them demands a different stance toward other people. Thus far in this book we have argued that such a stance could be gradually learned by (1) permitting oneself to be puzzled by and move toward discrepancies, (2) examining one's specific actions, thoughts, and feelings for the assumptions that guided the actions, thoughts, and feelings, (3) becoming less frightened by signs in others of emotions a leader has denied to himself, and (4) using one's intellect less to defend against indications of imperfections and more to inquire into the once-threatening information for the purpose of learning.

In the case of Joe we see that learning extended further. Now, not only is the learner less preoccupied with denying or defending (Joe's early stance of fatherly helper was a way of defending himself), he appears to turn around and extend his intellect toward another by imagining how Andy feels in his conflict with the Assistant Superintendent. In his questioning of Andy, we observe Joe using the group leader's guidelines to ask some very simple but quite sophisticated questions. The two sets of guidelines included:

Ask what happened, observably and internally.

Assume not a deficiency but a search, and listen closely to the choice of words and accompanying tone or feeling.

Ask oneself what the information shared thus far means to the speaker.

Ask for the specific words actually spoken in the exchange being described.

Listen for cues as to particular points of concern in the exchange.

Check to see if the identified points of concern match those of the speaker.

Invite speaker to recount what he was thinking and feeling at a particular point of concern in the exchange.

Imagine out loud what assumptions might give rise to the thoughts and feelings.

Joe's stature and confidence are in part reflected in his capacity to use the guidelines in his own way. (He has no need either to argue about them or to sit back and wait for somebody else to take the initiative.) Joe does the following:

Focuses simultaneously on Andy's effort to make sense and on Andy's concern by saying, "Andy, I thought that what bothered you was when the Assistant 'blew his top.'"

Calls attention back to Andy when it leaves him.

Asks, "What did the Assistant say actually . . .?"

Says, "You didn't like what you said, did you?"

Asks, "What didn't you like?"

Turns to group leader, indicating he's lost.

Acknowledges that he is lost.

States what he hears to be Andy's assumption, "So, maybe you say to yourself, if I really told my assistant all the negative information, I'd lose him for sure . . . if he blew up when I 'did nothing,' then disaster would result—?"

That these questions succeed in helping Andy seems apparent from the way in which Andy appears to feel recognized, is able then to reveal and examine his own discouragement, and finally appears to be ready to try once more to work with his assistant more effectively. Another way of looking at this sequence is that at the beginning of the fourth meeting, the tone and manner in which Andy told of the "blow up" with his assistant suggested that Andy took no responsibility for what happened. He was clearly upset that the situation had occurred, but he was describing the situation as if the Assistant were crazy. From the perspective of the other guy being at fault, there is no impetus for Andy to invent new, more effective behavior. Yet by the end of the meeting, Andy tentatively takes responsibility for his own limitations, his own faults, by setting out to invent some new behavior for attempting to interact more effectively with the Assistant.

It is not at all surprising, as he gets closer to the possibility of actually doing something different in the real setting of his school, that Andy encounters his ambivalence about the job itself. It is one thing to talk about what one might do, even to try out new behavior in a protected setting. It is quite another to anticipate the possible consequences of using new assumptions and behavior in one's real-world setting. Such anticipations, which often evoke negative consequences, heighten a person's natural ambivalence about change: Why should I? Will it be worth it? Can *I* really change? Won't I simply worsen the situation? These kinds of implicit and sometimes explicit questions bring forward in an individual the necessity for choice, commitment, and, in short, the taking of personal responsibility for one's actions. These are the themes upon which the final meeting concludes, as all the group members become involved, even several who were generally silent.

Joe Translates

The case we have just presented, then, illustrates:

A different model of helping (an inquiry model), contrasted with a more usual model (buck-up, advice-giving)

A learner emotionally confronting an assumption and doing so within a supportive environment

A learner trying out some new behavior in helping another person by using an inquiry model of helping

A learner attempting to translate new learnings by inventing new behaviors

A number of these ingredients in the case of Joe fit what we earlier defined as a phase of Translating. Translating, we suggested, was an organized phase of learning in which a learner attempts in a protected setting to create and test new forms of action which embody new assumptions. We also said that Translating focuses on interaction and on imagination. Its importance in learning stems from the premise that new insights do not easily translate into changed behavior. This is partly due to (1) the internal tensions between old and new patterns of behavior (2) the tensions between organizational demands for even performance and the unevenness of performance associated with learning, and (3) the tensions between the expectations which other people hold for appropriate leadership behavior and the new behavior of a leader based on new assumptions.

One way to examine these tensions is to look at the reception which people tend to get when they try out new behavior. The feelings that accompany attempted new behaviors tend to be anxiety, awkwardness, embarrassment, ambivalence. When trying out new behavior, people usually give mixed messages, appearing conflicted or extreme or insincere as they experience tensions between old and new patterns of behavior. Frequently these mixed messages raise similar feelings in others who, in response, experience fear or mistrust or anger. In fact, the behaviors of people who are changing tend to evoke in others precisely the kind of reaction that hinders and threatens change. The reactions can be portrayed as follows:

PERSON WHO IS CHANGING		PERSON RESPONDING	
Feels	*Acts*	*Feels*	*Acts*
Self-conscious	Awkward	Confused	Puts down/stifles
Angry	Defiant	Angry	Ignores
Ambivalent	Inconsistent	Ambivalent	Blindly approves
Fearful	Apologetic	Fearful	Advises/Corrects
Guilty		Guilty	
Mistrustful		Mistrustful	

When one attempts new behaviors in a protected setting, where attention can be paid to the conflicted and awkward feelings associated with the attempt, one has a better chance of inventing, practicing, and making one's own new ways of interacting with others. This in effect is what we see Joe do. He initially experiences the confusion of his own learning; appears to feel recognized when the group leader replays the initial help-giving episode, this time by legitimizing Joe's discouragement; and then attempts to offer a new kind of help to Andy.

The situation, of course, has been carefully structured by the group leader, concrete guidelines have been twice established, and the group leader is available when Joe gets stuck. In this sense, the episode does not represent the risks inherent in a real-world interaction. Yet Joe's behavior does represent a step forward from what we saw Steve doing in the previous case, where the situation was private and confidential, the threatening teacher at some safe distance, and the task an imaginary one of creating what he would say when confronting the teacher. Here Joe, in front of his peers, face-to-face with Andy, attempts to translate an experience of being helped and a concept about helping into actual questions, statements, and actions.

Another perspective on the tensions operating as a leader attempts to translate is provided by the leader's anticipation of the real world expectations for appropriate leadership behavior. The expectations for leadership were partially spelled out in Steve's case as he became clear about the components of "right and responsible leadership." (They will be developed further in Lew's case.) These included:

Show control of the situation.

Protect yourself, don't be vulnerable.

Act, don't think.

Act fast, get quick and decisive solutions.

Solve all, not part, of the problem.*

The central negative consequence of behaving according to these expectations is that they preclude the possibility of personal and interpersonal learning. Yet they are the general expectations with which a leader must contend as he acts from new assumptions about the value of learning. This conflict between old expectations and new assumptions is one more tension which a leader faces in trying to invent new behavior. Again, the existence of a protected setting in the form of a group committed to learning is an important support in working through this tension.

*This list is similar to the "governing variables" for interpersonal behavior which Argyris and Schön find controlling most interactions, in *Theory in Practice,* Jossey-Bass, 1974, pp. 66–72.

11 | A Theory of Interactive Learning

Introduction

The theoretical discussion which follows may at first prove puzzling to administrators in its use of the word "consultant." The reader may well ask what consultants have to do with a focus on the learning of leaders.

There are two answers to this question. The first is that in the learning pictured thus far, the consultant has been an important participant. That learning has occurred in and through an interaction. The person creating the conditions for that interaction has been the consultant. It is, therefore, important to understand the consultant's perspective.

The second reason for focusing on the consultant is that the consultant's framework for viewing interaction provides a useful model to leaders who want to think more systematically about their own interactions.

The focus of the preceding two cases (Steve and Joe) was on how learning occurs as framed by the consultant's perspective, just as the focus of the first two cases (Tom and Paul) was on what learning looks like as framed by the learner's perspective. In terms of the six learning phases, Tom's and Paul's cases encompassed the gamut, from starting points to action, while Steve's and Joe's focused on the specific phases in which the consultant plays a role: Examining Practice, Making New Sense, and Translating.

114

Lying behind those learning phases and informing the actions of the consultant is a theory of human learning. With four cases of learning to draw upon as examples of that theory in action, we intend at this point to engage in a theoretical discussion.

The starting point for the theory of learning lies in an assumption of human ambivalence.* One way of picturing that ambivalence is in terms of feelings about change: a wish for stability and permanence, on the one hand, and a wish for adventure on the other. People move back and forth between those poles. This ambivalence plays itself out, among other ways, in terms of a hope that someone else will provide the way to make "sense" of one's own experience and simultaneously the wish to make sense for oneself.

Steve's experience can be seen as expressive of this ambivalence about change. He moves back and forth between wanting to retain his image of strong and responsible leadership and at the same time attending to the voices of his past experience which are at odds with his image and which pull him toward making new sense.

The consultant takes on the task of helping nurture the part of the person that wants to increase his capacity to make his own sense, to take charge of his own fate. That part is tentatively willing to risk an attempt to shift the balance in the direction of change and to face the fear that comes with change.

One of the most vivid examples of a leader's moving toward risk taking can be found in Joe's case where, in the last group meeting, Andy shifts from his initial assertion that the problem he is experiencing lies entirely in the behavior of his assistant principal to the acknowledgement that he, Andy, no longer enjoys his job. This shift can be seen as a response to a set of conditions created by the consultant, which encourage participants to take the risks inherent in the idea of change.

To nurture the risk-taking part of a learner, we believe the consultant must embrace the whole person; to strengthen the part of a person that would risk change, the consultant must also honor the part that would resist change; to nurture a learner's new attempts to make sense of his experience, the consultant must simultaneously honor the old ways in which the learner made sense. Old assumptions constitute both an essential part of the learner's past efforts to take charge of his life and his present capacity to make order of life's chaos. It can feel to the learner that without the old assumptions he would cease to exist. From this perspective the old assumptions are cherished possessions. It appears that Paul feels this way when he repeatedly and angrily asserts that the behavior of others made "no sense." To offer help in such a way as to demean these old assumptions (no matter how limited they may be)

*Kiyo Morimoto, unpublished manuscript, *The Context for Learning.*

is to diminish the learner's confidence in his capacity to make sense and to reinforce that part of the learner which yearns for someone else to provide the answers. Help offered in a way that disparages past efforts to make sense confirms in a learner that part of himself that would be passive. Help of this sort is, therefore, negatively confirming.

Negative confirmation thus results from defining the learner in terms of what he lacks; engaging in the activities which attempt to get the learner out of the deficiency he is in; and producing the internal reaction in the learner of feeling bad, stupid, slow, or weak. The consequence is that the learner may feel he cannot make sense for himself and must rely on superior beings. When the learner feels negatively confirmed and is offered a different perspective on his situation, he may experience the new information as an obligation rather than as an alternative he might choose to try out.

The best example of this idea of negative confirmation can be found in the lists of helping behavior, assumptions, and hoped-for outcomes that the group in Joe's case develops with the consultant's help (pages 81 and 82).

Help based on the premise of a person's deficiencies is also likely to generate resistance. The resistance will frequently be perceived by the helper as further confirmation of the person's stupidity, weakness, and unwilling-ness to change. For example, when Joe did not find the group's help useful, his resistance to the group tended to generate impatience, anger, and confusion, which were expressed in a tone of "what's the matter with you, Joe?"

Positive confirmation, on the other hand, results from defining the learner in terms of what is there and engaging in the activities of acknowledging and legitimizing his assumptions. Acknowledgement produces the internal reaction in a learner of feeling recognized for what he is. Recognition for what he is produces the consequence of making the learner more receptive to new perspectives. New perspectives help him see the limits of his old assumptions and make him more receptive to still further new perspectives. Now the learner is in a position to respond to new information by choosing freely to explore, test, and use it.

Positive confirmation may involve statements normally perceived as positive as when the consultant offers Steve a different perspective on his confusion, "You wouldn't be confused if you didn't care." Positive confirmation can also involve statements normally perceived as outrageously negative as when the consultant says to Joe, "You were a flop."

From the perspective of positive confirmation, a learner's resistance can be seen not as further evidence of his stupidity but rather as an expression of his integrity—of his commitment to his old assumption as the best that, so far, he has available. For instance, Joe's resistance to the group's efforts to help him can be seen clearly as a sign of his integrity, not his intransigence. The concept of ambivalence, then, is central to the theory of interactive learning. It has profound implications for the ways in which help is offered and received.

What has just been said about ambivalence and positive confirmation also provides a framework for further understanding of the theme of confusion which appears in all four cases. Each of the learners has the experience of not being able to make sense in a situation even though he is not consciously aware that he is not able to make sense. He may, like Paul, use the words "it makes no sense," but his actions suggest that he does not fully feel that confusion is his problem. His perception seems based in an assumption that the world can be divided into two categories when things go wrong. Those two categories are that (1) there is something wrong with the situation or the other person or (2) there is something wrong with him. When what occurs cannot be fitted into either category, the leader, Paul, for example, gets confused. The confusion is experienced as a sign of his weakness, yet the confusion can be the key to discovering his assumption that the world can be divided into only two parts. Experienced as a weakness, confusion is something the leader must rid himself of in an effort to protect his cherished assumption, even as that assumption causes the confusion in the first place.

How can he experience his confusion as an invitation, thereby gain access to his old assumption and possibly entertain a different assumption which would allow him to make "better" sense? We believe that the key here is "recognition," a theme evident throughout the book.

The internal experience of being recognized is powerful. To be recognized by another person is to be granted the right to feel and think something that previously was "off limits." To have the right to think and feel the unthinkable—confusion, for example—is a first and necessary step toward taking responsibility for a part of the self (confusion, in particular) previously denied. One cannot take responsibility for that to which one feels one has no right.

Recognition by another person, then, enables a leader first to claim thoughts and feelings which were unthinkable and unfeelable, and thereby open the door to using them as access to the assumptions about self and others from which they follow. In short, recognition allows confusion to be experienced and learned from. The missing step in the theoretical sequence involves the reasons for the power of recognition in enabling people to learn. Those reasons cluster around the concept of perfection.

We argue that the reason the leaders in our cases had such limited ways of thinking about certain feelings and thoughts was that they believed they should not have them. The reason they believed they should not have those feelings and thoughts is that the existence of such emotions and thoughts was evidence of imperfection. From the point of view of being perfect, those unacceptable parts were enemies. They were enemies because their very existence was proof that the four leaders were not what they aspired to be in their own eyes: perfect. We believe that the hope that lies behind the goal of perfection is to be totally recognized and loved for one's whole self, even for those parts that one deems unacceptable. As one encounters the experience of having those "unacceptable" parts recognized and welcomed into legitimate participation within the whole self, as one experiences being recognized not for being perfect but for being "imperfect," one becomes able to relinquish gradually one's need to be perfect.

Allowing oneself to be recognized for one's "imperfections" can lead to a redefinition of what it means to be human. That different definition involves not perfection but wholeness. According to this definition, one does not grow by continually perfecting or adding on to the "good" parts of oneself and suppressing or eliminating the "bad." Instead, one grows by integrating all the parts. Integration involves coming to recognize and welcome unknown parts, inquiring into them, and finally coming to accept them.

As we saw in the case of Steve, integration of the parts of the self brings with it an increase in the amount and kind of information available. Steve becomes conscious of his confusion, of the view he holds of himself for being confused—"he's a jerk," and he allows himself to bring on-limits his wish for an easy way out of his jam. The act of bringing on-limits this new information has the effect of generating other new information. For Steve to recognize that he has seen himself as a "jerk" is to ask, "Am I? Why? Maybe not." To wish fully to escape can open Steve to recognition that he wants to stay and work "it" out. This is new information.

As the parts of the self become increasingly integrated, less of the person's intellect has to be directed at getting rid of the parts felt to be "enemies." We saw Steve, Joe, and Andy go through making "friends" of parts of themselves which they felt to be "enemies"—Steve's confusion, Joe's fear, Andy's disappointment and doubt—and experience a sense of release, openness to new perspectives from others, rebirth of hope, and a desire to engage again with those people with whom they had difficulty.

This desire for renewed interaction occurs because as a person's intellect becomes less preoccupied with warding off internal "enemies," it becomes more available for different kinds of use. An apparently spontaneous and natural expression of the person's freed-up intellect is curiosity about other people as separate, unique persons who make sense of the world according to a different set of assumptions. Others are seen less as potential threats to the person's self and image of "right and responsible leadership," and more as potential learners.

A curiosity about others, combined with a sense of humility and respect which comes from embracing one's own "imperfections" can, through practice, become the discipline of empathy. Empathy is the cornerstone of how we believe a person himself grows and enables others to grow. In Paul's interaction with the parent, and, in particular with the teacher, we saw pictures of empathic behavior. Likewise, we saw the consultant extend himself empathically with Steve and Joe, Sam extend himself with Joe, and Joe extend himself with Andy.

Many people believe empathy for, and identifying with, another person are the same thing. For example, many of the administrators in the Joe case might think of their "buck-up behavior" as empathic behavior. We see their behavior not as empathic but as identifying. Their behavior seems predicated on the assumption that: If I were *in* what he (Joe) is, I'd want to be *out*; therefore, I will try to help him *out.* Identifying behavior follows from an assumption that people are the same.

By contrast, empathy is an extension of intellect to another person, based on the knowledge that each person is different and separate. (Paul calls this "crossing the great divide.") Empathy is based on a rigorous discipline of a person caring for his own feelings and thoughts (enabled through being *recognized*) so that he can attend to what the other person *might* be experiencing, and he can test his assumptions about what the other is experiencing rather than act from his assumptions before testing them. When a leader can hear and recognize the other person, that person is able to take personal responsibility for his feelings and thoughts, which in turn leads to different, less defensive behavior.

Identification, on the other hand, because it assumes that a leader already knows what the other is thinking and feeling, does not encourage the leader to test his assumptions about the other person's experience and tends to have the consequence of not recognizing the other, leaving the other unheard and more defensive than before.

The movement from discrepancies through personal recognition to empathy as a discipline central to taking new action is what we mean by learning in this book.

The learning phases we have used are ways of describing what happens. To repeat what we have just said in terms of those phases: The context changes in some way upsetting the previous balance between the wish for permanence and stability and the wish for adventure and change. The combination of pain and the individual's wish to make sense of his own life may cause him to recognize a *starting point*, to acknowledge a discrepancy, to become aware that he cannot make sense. By *examining practice* with the help of someone who legitimizes ambivalence, the learner welcomes unknown parts of the self into existence and thereby encounters the assumptions he makes.

Through recognition of the varied parts of the self, the learner begins to *make new sense.* What before he saw as enemies within, he begins to see as potential friends. Hence he can continue his effort to make new sense by seeking out and considering the new perspectives offered by the consultant. The consultant can offer his views without fear of their being negatively confirming.

With new assumptions available on which to base new behavior, the learner now tries to *translate* his new sense into new forms of action by inventing and testing new behaviors in a protected setting designed to give him careful feedback. As he becomes skilled at inventing new behavior, he becomes increasingly ready to strike out on his own and *take new action*.

While this learning sequence is often the one followed, it is not the only one. For example, some people start by examining their practice and then discover discrepancies. Others, when engaged in translating new forms of thought and feeling into new behavior, discover assumptions they did not know they held.

Summary

In this chapter we have attempted to offer a theoretical explanation for the learning pictured in the cases in this book.* The learning has resulted in increased competency in interactive situations. We believe this learning is most likely to occur through interactions. The essence of that interactive learning is based on the concept of ambivalence.

By being recognized for all of one's conflicting parts and for one's efforts to make sense, a learner is able to welcome parts of the self of which he was previously unaware because their existence threatened the desire to be perfect and thus loved. Once fully accepted, those parts can also be relinquished, and new expanded ways of feeling and thought can be freely chosen.

In the final case we will see how a leader takes action after experiencing learning of the sort described here and illustrated in the preceding cases.

*In offering this theoretical explanation, we are heavily indebted to the work of Kiyo Morimoto. Central to the theory presented here are his concepts of negative and positive confirmation; perfection and wholeness and recognition (though he would call it "acknowledgment"), as well as his concept of ambivalence. We have interpreted these concepts in our own way and take full responsibility for them.

Part 4 | A LEARNER WHO LEADS

In the final case in the book, a leader consciously and directly uses his learning to transform his leadership style. His changed performance helps a subordinate become more effective. The leader has engaged in repeated interactions with an individual consultant and with a group over a period of four years.

Not only has the leader interacted with the consultant and other leaders and changed his ways of thinking and leading, but he has also become interested in, and has committed himself to, the study of the theory of interactive learning (Chapter 11). Where that theory was set forth in terms of a framework which a consultant would use in helping an administrator to learn in a protected setting, here we see its adaptation by a leader who uses it in a professional setting to help a subordinate learn.

12 | Lew's Case

As we come to Lew at the end of the book, we encounter a situation remarkably similar to Tom's at the book's beginning. As in Tom's case, Lew has had a history of interpersonal conflict with the teacher he confronts, although in Lew's case the history of conflict is longer. As in Tom's case, the solution to the problem is similar, namely moving the teacher to another grade, and again, as in Tom's case, Lew's success generated interest on the part of another leader in the system.

The similarities in the cases, while coincidental in reality, are deliberately maintained, for they highlight the extraordinary extent to which Lew has carried his learning: He succeeds in doing with Helen what Tom hoped to accomplish with Lynn but did not yet have the framework or skills to achieve.

Lew's case is different from the others in this book in that Lew's story incorporates italicized portions which were inserted after the narrative was completed. The italicized material was formulated jointly by Lew and the consultant in an effort to account for some of the thinking which might have influenced Lew in the moment to act as he did. The italicized material does not represent Lew's actual thoughts at the time of the action but rather an articulation of his hunches or instincts about what might have led him to act as he did in the moments of action.

Lew is different from the other characters in this book in another way. He speaks, particularly at the beginning of the case, from a persona, a cocky, needling show-off voice. This voice was more central to his personality ten years earlier than it is now, but Lew resorts to it as he describes himself in that earlier period and then tends to drop it as the narrative progresses in time and in terms of his own development.

"YOU MAY WIND UP THINKING SOMETHING CAN BE DONE"

I hated that T-group fad of the late sixties and early seventies. When I came here in '69, quite a few of the teachers were "into," as they said, the human potential movement.

Their exposure to "the movement" seemed to account, at the time, for Helen's outrageous behavior. Of course, Helen, a second grade teacher in the school, had gone on tenure the year before I came, so the security of her new position may have contributed to her daring to "confront" me. It was quite a welcome, I'll tell you.

I was here two, maybe three, months (in my second principalship; this locale was new, but the principalship wasn't) when Helen came to me with a problem. She said that the curriculum coordinator was incompetent, and I had "better do something about it." As Helen told how the curriculum coordinator was sowing seeds of the school's destruction, she spoke in such a secretive yet demanding manner that I had a difficult time taking her seriously. She closed her presentation with dramatic flair.

"I can no longer tolerate this man in my room," she declared, with a pause apparently timed to give drama to a final clincher, "and many other teachers feel this way, too." Of course, I could get no numbers or names of other disgruntled faculty members. I didn't need numbers or names, Helen assured me. I needed only to trust the validity of her data and conclusions.

When this meeting ended, two weeks passed before Helen and I met again. At this second meeting I found that Helen's version of our first meeting was quite different from mine. She remembered me advising her that:

1. She should go through proper channels. In short, she should speak to the curriculum coordinator before coming to me.
2. She should not be afraid of giving negative feedback to the curriculum coordinator.
3. She should not take her differences with the curriculum coordinator so

"personally"; instead she should stay focused on the issue, stay problem-centered.
4.   She should bellyache less and act more to solve the problem.

This high-quality advice is printed indelibly in my mind because Helen had written it down, and she literally read it back to me in our second meeting.

The background circumstances to this second meeting were these: There is a makeshift wall between my office and the teachers' room. One afternoon late, I was in my office complaining to an assistant super about my assistant principal. The next day, Helen made an appointment to see me and, when she arrived, revealed that coincidentally she had been in the teachers' room the afternoon before.

Much abbreviated, the following is the "confrontation" Helen "laid on" me:

HELEN: "Didn't you break channels by speaking with the assistant super before talking with your assistant principal?"
(me) LEW: "Yes . . . I guess so."
HELEN: "Yet you advised me to go through proper channels."

HELEN: "Did you give negative feedback to your assistant?"
LEW: "No, but you don't understand what's at stake here . . ."
HELEN: "Yet you advised me not to be afraid of giving negative feedback."

HELEN: "Didn't the assistant super feel that you were taking the actions of your assistant personally, and overreacting? You failed to stay focused on the issues, didn't you?"
LEW: "What is this? An inquisition? You had no business making this your business in the first place."
HELEN: "Yet you faulted me for taking the curriculum coordinator personally (not staying problem-centered)."

HELEN: "So, in effect, you were complaining but doing nothing."
LEW: "This is a difficult situation, I'm afraid. You have no idea what's going on."
HELEN: But, the point is, you told me to stop complaining and act."

No contest. Actually, my reaction to her at the time, nine years ago, differs from now. Then, I didn't know what to make of her outrageous behavior, except that it was way out of line. I'd heard Helen was a bit of a crank, and this proved it. To me, her conflict with the curriculum coordinator differed from my difficulty with my assistant. I saw my assistant as having outlived his usefulness, but the curriculum coordinator seemed a competent professional to me. The cause of Helen's behavior seemed to lie in her exposure to T-group confrontation before I came.

In the remaining months of that first year, I had no significant contact with Helen. I did find out more about her, though. She used the language of "confrontation," but her participation in the T-group activities before I came was minimal. When she did attend, she did not get involved. More important, the previous principal had doubts about recommending her for tenure but was stuck with his own too-positive evaluations. Each of the three years he evaluated her he wrote under "Areas for Improvement"—"needs more flexibility in applying expectations for performance." Terrific stuff. The meaning of this obfuscation came clear during the next few years.

In short, during those next few years and the years to date, I received lots of parent complaints and faculty complaints about Helen, saying that she marched to the beat of her own drummer. She listened to no one and spoke the truth to all—children, parents, faculty, and to me. The specifics of these complaints and my assessment of Helen's teaching will come up later when I tell about the set of conversations which recently occurred between Helen and me after nine years.

The real significance of Helen in this story is as catalyst in, focus for, and finally a test of my own attempts to improve my leadership, particularly in the area of evaluation and supervision, so, unfortunately, I'll end up using Helen more as a foil than as a whole person. My aim here is to show how after eight years of dancing with Helen to the tune of "You don't give me any trouble, I'll return the favor," I finally began to work with her directly in a way which has resulted in growth for both of us.

No small accomplishment. Helen is a tough cookie. As it turns out, there have been several other teachers here since the time of the T-group who, like Helen, took it upon themselves to educate me. They called themselves the "Hippie Fringe."

This small group of converts to confrontation designed the "Principal Bullshit Scale." I ranked high in several ways. It seems:

1. I had "a habit of pointing out and condemning sarcasm when used by teachers on children," but little awareness about my use of it on teachers and its negative consequences.
2. I gave lots of advice but didn't take it gracefully.
3. I had a set of habitual behaviors described as, "A teacher will hardly finish a statement and immediately he puts forth a counterargument, an explanation, a sarcastic barb, or a solution to an assumed problem, and considers himself helpful in doing so."
4. I was described as, "He shows his tail in the face of concerted resistance,

or he takes unilateral, arbitrary stands as a show of strength." The quotes are a result of my "liberating" (after four years on the job) a copy of the infamous "Scale."

There seemed no end to theatrics during those first few years, though in retrospect I realize that these few individuals, the Hippie Fringe, pointed out my foibles in reasonably decent ways, which I tried to dismiss much as I dismissed the information from Helen's "confrontation." Still, the "feedback" had a way of nagging at me occasionally. Much to my surprise, the feedback became useful to me in the fall of 1973 as a consequence of an important conclusion I came to: The future necessity and challenge to administrators lay in the area of evaluation/supervision.

What I'd seen coming, gradually, in my school system and others, as well as in the general social scene, was the end of expansion. Enrollments were beginning to drop. Taxpayers were becoming unwilling to fork over more to pay for less. There were "bad vibes" from the public about the "quality of education"—meaning, get back to those "basics." At meetings run by central office personnel, the theme had become, Cut Back.

So that fall of my fifth year in this school I joined a leadership training program, where I focused my "study" on evaluation and supervision, though these activities proved only the vehicle for a larger look at how I lead. Gradually, and then explosively, the information from Helen and the Hippie Fringe became a crucial tool for my growth.

I've been in this leadership program for more than four years now. It's an old tale of woe—you go into the shop with a busted taillight and find out that the whole electrical system is fouled up. But I plan to spare myself a lengthy journey back through the questions I asked and tried to answer during these years.

Very briefly, some of those questions were, How did I get into this business? Why? Do I really want to be here? What makes me think of myself as a leader? Am I really interested in changing my performance? Is it possible to change? Why should I? How do I account for the massive discrepancy between how I see myself and how I'm seen in action by others? So what? Why should I take seriously what they say? What do I really care about? Do I lead by the priorities of what I care about? Why not?

What's the verdict? An adolescent crisis, twenty-five years too late? Who knows, in the end? Here's a quick chronology of my years studying my own leadership through participation in learning groups with other administrators and regular work with an outside consultant:

First year: Thank goodness, other administrators
(fall 1974)   have problems, too.

(winter 1974)	I thought I had problems, but there are administrators with worse problems than mine.
(spring 1974)	I take back what I said about the other administrators; I'm worse off than I knew.
Second year: (fall 1975)	So Helen and the Hippie Fringe were right about my foibles, but I wonder if they are learning, as I am, that confrontation doesn't have to mean behaving outrageously toward others; the School Committee has decreed that in two years *all* teachers will be evaluated.
Third year: (fall 1976)	The major event of my learning is a confrontation with Jane.
Fourth year: (fall 1977)	I finally face myself and Helen, and we come out the better for it.

Imagine my embarrassment during these years as my own study took me into that territory I considered T-group heaven: There was the land of "Get to Know Yourself" with its capital, "Examine Your Professional Practice." The inhabitants of this capital went by foreign names, strangely interrelated: There was a character named "What You Say You Do" who was related to, but quite different from, another character, "What You Do Do," as illustrated in videotapes, audiotapes or case descriptions of your work.

Then there were "Thoughts" and "Feelings," which go on while you act, and an examination of them reveals a disturbing character, "Assumptions," who carries a lot of weight when it comes to how you lead. This "Assumptions" character is hard to get to know because he often has a very different version of what you're doing than what you think you're doing at the time.

In short, during the first three years of my study I found that I had a set of unknown assumptions which guided my interpersonal actions as a leader and which contrasted sharply with how I thought about my leadership.

ASSUMPTIONS GUIDING MY ACTIONS AS A LEADER	HOW I THOUGHT ABOUT MY ACTIONS
If I am to lead effectively, then I must be:	
right	I am:
liked	helpful
in control	respected
invulnerable	efficient, firm
rational (no feelings)	open
	considerate

So what? I was busy trying to be right, liked, in control, invulnerable, and rational in my contact with people. But I did not know that these criteria were guiding my actions. "Say, like, man, you are out of touch," one friendly "fringe" person told me. He didn't stay long on the faculty, for reasons of his own, though I was hardly sorry to see him go. The point is that I was saying one thing and doing another. This lowered my "credibility" with the faculty.

More importantly, since I saw myself as a finished product, I didn't need to learn. Teach others—yes; learn myself—no. So what? As I said before, I saw the future of administration in the area of evaluation/supervision; in *growth*, to put it in a word. As a result of Helen's provocation and feedback from the Hippie Fringe about my performance, I'd gotten an inkling that I was missing out on something, that there were forces in me and others which when it came to growing, held the upper hand. Inner life forces, of which I was not well acquainted. Publicly, I declared this the territory of an occasional "fringe" person and mushy-minded psychologists. Privately, I was intrigued.

Rather than speak generally about my journey into these inner life forces, I want to see if I can insert the results of that journey into dialogue with a teacher, Jane, where I see my leading different than in the past. Indeed, I see my efforts here with Jane and later with Helen as a redefinition of how I lead, in practical terms of where I put my time and focus my energies—on my growth and the growth of individual members of my staff.

Early in the academic year 1975–76, during the third year of my study, I had a chance meeting with Jane, a fourth grade teacher, which solidified much of what I'd been studying and allowed a crucial new insight into my assumptions about growth. Jane has different values than I do, a different way of seeing things. She's one of those teachers I shy away from, for the very reason that I'd come to negative conclusions about her and she about me. It's one thing to give and take negative information from someone who trusts and likes me and vice versa. It's an entirely different matter with someone who mistrusts me and may not like me, and the other way around.

Jane mistrusted me and seemed not to like me, and I felt the same toward her. In this very important way Jane was like Helen, and the conflict between Jane and me was a turning point in preparing me for the upcoming conflict with Helen. In fact, without this incident of conflict with Jane, I don't think I'd have had enough *hope* to persevere with Helen. *Hope*, that's right; hope was like a picture inside me of what could be possible. Hope that, contrary to my instincts, positive results can come with painful conflict.

Though Jane and Helen were similar, they were very different, at the same time, in relation to me. Helen was ten to fifteen years older than me; Jane was about my age, just-forties. Where Helen had taught in the school for thirteen years, Jane had been transferred here only a year and a half before this meeting. Where Helen was rigidly nontraditional in her teaching, Jane was rigidly traditional.

For the year and a half Jane spent in the school before this meeting, we had a superficial relationship. We were no more than polite to each other. As I saw her, she was rigid and inflexible in her relationships with both staff and students. She ran a traditional classroom, very structured, and had very high expectations of children's behavior. The big discussion every year was whether or not children were allowed to wear hats in school.

She would emotionally put a child in a corner and wouldn't let him out of that corner until he either backed down or croaked. So the child either had the choice of croaking in front of all the kids or being defiant to her, one or the other. Certain children wouldn't give in. They'd become defiant to her, and this she couldn't tolerate and she would lose all control. She felt very strongly that the principal should be someone to fear, that everyone fears—kids and teachers—so, she did not like the way I disciplined children.

After school about three o'clock one day I was walking down the hallway to see another teacher. Jane stopped me and told me about what some child had done and said, "You should do something about that."

I said, "What do you want me to do?"

"Well," she retorted, "Expel him, or suspend him, or something."

Instead of countering Jane's retort with a statement like, "You'd be better off attending to your teaching than complaining about my discipline of children," I forced myself to try something I'd practiced again and again in my learning groups called "listening nonliterally" and "imagining out loud." These are very difficult activities of mind and action. They are terribly cumbersome and self-conscious at first, but after lots of practice, I got easier with them. These activities require that I:

1. *Recognize and break my reflex to jump in and simply counterpunch what the other person said ("You'd be better off attending to your teaching than complaining about my discipline of children").*
2. *Recognize what I think the other person said which I reflexively took to reflect badly on me (I haven't done "something," and I should have).*
3. *Set aside that literal reading of what the other person said, and ask myself, "What concern could that person be expressing in this ("You do something now!) particular way?" or, "What entrapping situation could that person be in which would lead to this particular form of expression?" (I thought Jane was saying that she wanted something done but didn't trust me to do it.)*
4. *Formulate a way of "imagining out loud" what concern or situation I think the other person is expressing.*

My attempt to imagine out loud came out as, "You don't trust me to handle this situation properly?"

Jane snapped, "No," then stopped, and hesitantly continued, "No, it's not a matter of trust." She paused, collecting her thoughts, "It's that you don't back up your teachers!" She paused again, apparently intending to continue.

One aim of "listening nonliterally" and "imagining out loud" is to ask the other person to slow down, to think about what they are saying, such that the two of us might take time to mutually define the problem before rushing to solution. It seemed to me that my attempt to imagine out loud had forced Jane to stop and think about what she was saying and allowed me to get new information about what might concern her.

When it became apparent that she was not going to continue, I said defensively, "I do want to back up teachers, but not at the expense of children's learning."

Jane began right away, "You aren't doing children any service, let me tell you!"

I was angry, "Have you ever stopped to think about why I talk to children in a hopefully nonthreatening way?"

Jane didn't speak right away, so I went on, "Would you listen if I tried to explain?" She said she would, reluctantly, so I asked her to sit with me in her room.

After some discussion of discipline, we somehow switched to relationships between faculty members and between the faculty and me. At about this time I began to feel that this unexpected event was, well, propelling me into something dangerous and yet inviting. Later I realized that the unexpectedness of the event itself made the conflict possible; I never would have planned to get involved in this way with Jane.

When Jane speaks at a staff meeting, usually very negatively and cuttingly, other members of the staff resent her tone and counter her arguments with other arguments. I explained this pattern of interaction to her as I've seen it and others see it, too.

"They don't respect me," she said, bitterly. I told her that the other teachers thought that she didn't respect them and that that's why they act toward her the way they do.

"They feel that you don't give them the courtesy of being professional," I told her. She was shocked.

"And," I said, "furthermore, Jane, some of them don't think that you respect me. And I don't think you do either."

She was shocked again, and exclaimed, "I never knew that." Like the lightning bolt had struck her, she hung in silence on her own words.

Of course there was no explicit way she could have known these views because I'd never risked telling her this negative information. She wanted to know how I could possibly come to such a conclusion, so I told her, describing concretely what I'd seen her do, and what the consequences of her actions were to me and to others. Before long we were focused on my negative conclusions about her teaching.

I told her that I saw her overcontrolling her classroom and trapping kids, and we spent two hours trying to see why she did this and how she could change, because it turned out she didn't like what was going on.

Before we finished, she forced the discussion back to discipline. At first, she raked me over the coals again for not maintaining a clearer, firmer policy and practice. She might have continued a generalized diatribe which simply resulted in my getting more and more defensive, if I had not forced myself to try a second new set of skills aimed at producing the conditions for dialogue and growth through dialogue. These skills go hand in hand with "listening nonliterally" and "imagining out loud." This second set of skills are called "translating back" and "putting yourself on the map."

Jane was saying, "You don't see that you pamper kids in the name of kindness, and—"

I interrupted. "Jane, I'm having an awful time listening to you because I can't make sense of what you're saying. I am at a loss . . . *lost!*" As I "put myself on the map," my mind cleared a bit, and I was able to tell her more about my dilemma and how she might help me.

"I find myself torn between simply telling you you're wrong and trying to learn from what you say. . . . Your repeated use of words like *pamper, coddle, hand-hold* simply anger me. . . . Maybe if we could take one specific child and look at what I actually did by way of discipline . . . maybe that would help me. . . ."

Jane agreed, and we constructed a step-by-step chronology of how I handled one student she'd sent to me several times. With the help of my continued attempts to put myself on the map, particularly in terms of what was helpful and not helpful, Jane supplied information about the consequences of my disciplinary actions, which were new to me and troubling. I told her so.

The skills of "translating back" and "putting yourself on the map" demand a set of activities of mind and action which can be as difficult as those in "listening nonliterally" and "imagining out loud." These activities require that I:

1. *Recognize the feelings produced in me by other people's behavior (anger, for example, at Jane's use of the words* pamper, coddle, *etc.).*

2. *Translate back from the feeling I recognize (anger) to prior or accompanying feelings by asking questions from a nonliteral perspective: "What has happened inside me which was a prior condition of my anger?" (Here, for example, I was hurt.) "What internal conditions, apart from the other person's behavior, account for my hurt?" (Here, for example, I wanted to understand what Jane was saying about my discipline of children, but I could not make sense—her view of my work was so much different from my view that her words were a mystery, a threatening one at that.)*

3. *Identify the concrete behavior by the other person which produces feelings in me (for example, Jane's repetition of abstract, emotionally laden words—pamper, coddle, etc.).*

4. *Put myself on the map by formulating a response which describes concretely the behavior of the other person and its consequences to me in feeling ("Your repeated use of words like pamper, coddle, hand-hold simply anger me . . ."), and try to tell the other person how he or she could offer information so that it would be useful ("Maybe if we could take one specific child and look at what I actually did by way of discipline . . .").*

As I see it, these skills of "translating back" and "putting myself on the map" are directed toward me; they allow me to search within for clarity and present myself as vulnerable, as related rather than alone in my search for meaning. In contrast, the skills of "listening nonliterally" and "imagining out loud" are directed toward the other person rather than me; they offer the other person a chance to search for clarity of thought and to experience himself as related rather than alone in his search for meaning. The trick for me is to find ways of using the two sets of skills in a balanced way which results in creating the possibility of learning for both people.

Jane and I talked for nearly three hours that afternoon. The next morning she broke into my office. She had to talk, "You know, I know why I do that now," referring to her overcontrolling her classroom and trapping kids into croaking or defying. During the night she had reflected on her own overcontrolled childhood and gotten some insights into the relationship between how she was brought up and how she taught. These insights were so exciting that she wanted to know of ways she could go further with them, in hopes of improving her teaching. I told her about my efforts to learn with the consultant and other principals, and referred her to other possible resources.

In the retelling, this discussion sounds like a fairy tale. It is unusually dramatic in consequence but no less true for that. Since this conversation I've had a very different relationship with Jane, much less superficial. I think she's better off as a result of our talk. She seems to be much more relaxed, although she's still uptight sometimes.

This interaction was a landmark to me. I had never had such an experience with a teacher. I was quite shaken—emotionally exhausted—at the end of it and excited that we were both able to take that risk of really confronting each other. It was very difficult because I said things to her, my negative assumptions, which I've never said so forthrightly to a teacher before, and she hurt but she didn't break. Quite the contrary, in fact. She learned. And, she said hard things to me which hurt. But I didn't break. I learned, too.

I learned in that I raised serious questions about how I discipline kids. I learned, too, about my own increasing ability to handle conflict, and its potential positive outcomes. Specifically, I found I could separate out what I thought was her stuff, her fears and projections onto me, and what were, in contrast, some good insights about me. Years before, in the episode with Helen, I did not have the capacity to do this. I could not actively engage in conversation with the purpose of separating out Helen's projections from my foibles. The only point of view I had was, "What's wrong with her?"

But most importantly, in this meeting with Jane, I learned how wrong I was about Jane's not wanting to learn. I had her written off as having "personality problems" too deep to change. I was dead wrong and, as a result, began to seriously question if other teachers didn't want to learn, too, even though it might not look that way to me.

In short, this meeting with Jane altered my perception radically. At a rational level I believed in the possibility of learning and growth. Education is my business, the business of learning and growth, but at an emotional level, I discovered a different and disturbing assumption: I doubted that people in general can change.

In my mind, I believed in the possibility of change, but I found that in my heart I did not believe. This meeting with Jane expanded my heart, like a long distance runner expands his lungs and strengthens his heart through training. This meeting with Jane was a necessary prelude to meeting with Helen. During the remainder of the year, I saw Jane get some outside help, engage another teacher in regular dialogue about their work in the classroom, and begin, slowly, to make herself into a better teacher.

The meeting with Jane occurred at the beginning of the academic year 1975–76. It wasn't until the beginning of the next year that I engaged Helen. During the year between these two confrontations, I went further in my study of myself as a leader; in particular, I pushed out in the direction of how to interact with others to create conditions for change and growth. In that regard, my efforts were guided by a quaint, seedy quote which implicitly put forward a radical theory about growth:

Living on a little requires genuine freedom of mind—meaning you've got to imagine otherness from within and see yourself from without—and push and push and push. Tricky job. Still, it's possible. You work piece by piece, elbows in, hands up. Stretch your head, don't waste time arguing and contradicting, look to learn, try to *find* the other fellow as he is known to himself. You'll be fascinated, wait and see. Life will seem absorbing, you may wind up thinking something can be done. *

Just reading that quote again reminds me of how uncomfortable I still can be with this content of my study. I mean, how about that—"imagine otherness from within and see yourself from without"—let alone this, "try to *find* the other fellow as he is known to himself." T-group heaven. Hardly a man's work. A man's work has more to do with "arguing and contradicting" than looking to learn. Sissy stuff. Hardly the hard administrative work of tasks, delegation, decision . . . being in charge.

Still, ironically, I think I'm more in charge of more of myself than ever, as a direct result of facing the unknown forces within me and learning to invite others to do the same, for themselves. I linger on this man-or-mouse business here because it was a big issue in sitting down with Helen, which I'm about to do—in a manner of speaking. I knew I would have to place myself much more at risk with Helen than I had with Jane. The meeting with Jane happened by accident and was essentially a one-shot deal. The work I had to do with Helen was consciously planned ahead of time and involved my setting up and following through on a series of highly unusual meetings with her.

What was at stake in meeting with Helen was my breaking lots of rules for appropriate relations between faculty and principal, rules which I'd been implicitly supporting for years. The School Committee edict that all teachers be evaluated gave me support in beginning to break some of these rules, but, for the most part, I was on my own in my effort to violate these rules with positive consequences. Some of these rules were:

Principal protects teachers from bad news rather than confronts with bad news.

Principal provides material resources and otherwise keeps out of teachers' classroom business unless asked.

Principal acts as problem solver, as in disciplining children, rather than as supervisor capable of helping teachers become better at disciplining children.

Life and the Student, Charles Horton Cooley, as quoted by Benjamin DeMott, *Supergrow*, E. P. Dutton, New York, 1969, p. 167.

From another perspective, that of assumptions about how to lead, I was, in meeting with Helen, consciously planning to violate, if possible, the assumptions which said that if I were to lead properly then I should:

Try to win or be in control through being right (with advice, answers, solutions, put downs, assigning blame and getting Helen to accept it) or through being liked (by not pushing too hard, staying on the positive side, reassuring, encouraging, patting on the back, "stroking").

Try to be invulnerable, through presenting myself as a finished product rather than a fallible, limited, incomplete, searching person.

Try to be rational, through presenting myself as moved by reason rather than feeling, as having a truth through logic which can prove feeling to be inconsequential, irrelevant, or unprofessional.

The First Meeting with Helen

As soon as Helen had settled into her routine for the year, perhaps two weeks had passed in the fall of 1976–77, I went to her room one day after school and told her I'd like to meet with her in the next week. I told her that the meeting was in preparation for the evaluations I'd be conducting later in the year. We were able to set a time for two days hence, after classes ended for the day.

When Helen arrived in my office, I was pumped up with anxiety, hesitant, and clumsy in asking her to take a seat and very deliberate as I began my long anticipated "confrontation."

"As you know, later this year I have to evaluate your performance. I thought that before we began that process, we might talk about our past history together, in an effort to clear the air.

"There are two aspects of our history I want to talk about. One, your initial confrontation with me eight years ago; two, my and other people's evaluations of your performance through the years.

"When I came here eight years ago, you 'confronted' me with the blatant contradiction between what I advised you to do about an interpersonal difficulty of yours and what I actually did in handling an interpersonal difficulty of mine; my actions belied my words of advice to you. Implicitly, you said I was a phony, a fraud—"

Helen began to interrupt, "I didn't tell you you were a fraud—"

"Not in so many words," I interjected. I was about to say, "You may not have told *me* in so many words, but you sure told others on the faculty," but luckily I caught myself getting sucked into an old pattern of one-upmanship and stopped.

I continued, "At the time I hardly knew what to make of your behavior, except to label it bizarre, write you off as a crank, and get on with other business."

Helen began to speak, and I asked her to wait until I finished. She acquiesced. I breathed a sigh of relief. I usually let her interrupt me.

"From our occasional conversations since, I realize that you saw yourself 'daring to be open' with me. In fact, now, I can imagine and believe you viewed your actions in that way—as a service to me. Now, I can also say that you hurt me and left me confused and angry. As you yourself have told me, I was for some time bitter about your spreading the story of my phoniness among members of the staff.

"Today, I look back and see what you did very differently from how I saw and reacted to it then. Now, I think you might have been hurt by the way I failed to pay attention to you and your problem with the curriculum coordinator. I gave you some cheap advice which might have registered as a reprimand and then I compounded the indignity by demonstrating in my own behavior that the advice was empty, as you already knew, perhaps.

"Ironically, I want to thank you for 'daring to be open' way-back-when because in retrospect the content of what you said put a crack in the shell of my thinking about who I am as a leader. That crack was widened by feedback from others which supported what you said about me and added to it: I was fat on advice and thin on acting according to it; I was fat with talk and thin on listening; fat on running things right but thin on putting myself in a position to learn.

"Actually, my point is that what you said, when combined with other similar information, has led me to try to change. For that information, I am thankful.

"I say all this in hopes of putting this part of our history to rest. If possible, I don't want it to cloud and confuse our evaluation sessions later this year."

Helen spoke immediately, "I've always thought you were biased against me because of that incident."

"I know," I replied, "and you have been right about my bias."

"It's all so long ago; this is silly to rehash . . ." Helen's voice began in a tone of rebuff and then trailed off.

I did not speak. It seemed to me that as she began to write off my remarks, some other thought or feeling had intruded itself into her consciousness, thus accounting for the trailing-off quality in her voice. I was curious to see if she would choose to speak that new thought.

She began again, slowly, "Though, I admit, even now I remember how I was bothered by the way you dismissed me so breezily with that advice. As if I were completely wacky."

"Wacky?" I said laughing, caught in surprise at her use of the word to describe herself.

"Yes, you just wrote me off with a simple, 'Helen, you are wrong. I am right. Go get your house in order.'"

"Indeed I did," I said. Helen seemed surprised, a bit discombobulated, actually. I waited a moment to give her a chance to speak, but she didn't. So I did.

"There's a second history I want to talk about today, and it has to do with information I've received from others about your work with children. Over the years I've made an attempt, half-hearted as it might appear from this vantage point, to inform you of parent concerns about the effect of your teaching on some children."

Helen jumped me, "And when you've done that I've spoken to the parents and cleared up the matter." She paused and began to continue, but I stopped her.

"Please, let me finish," I said firmly. Helen looked hurt.

My effort was to get the whole story out before disputing parts. The way I saw it, the whole was the message, more than any single one of the parts. Still, it was no small accomplishment for me to stop Helen and continue.

"But, I have withheld from you a great deal of negative information from parents, members of the staff, children, and me. I withheld the information on the assumption that I was acting in your best interest. I thought that if you heard this negative information, you would do a worse job rather than a better job.

"Now I see that I assumed you were weaker than I think you actually are. In fact, I was protecting myself, and I was patronizing and condescending to you, as indeed you have claimed in the past."

Helen had a look which seemed somewhere between quizzical and stunned, so I stopped for several seconds to give her a chance to speak. She waited. I went on.

"So, here's the whole picture. Over the past eight years there has been a steady increase in the number of parent requests to have children removed from your room and requests to *not* place children in your room. The number of requests for removal has gone from three the first year to as many as sixteen last year—sixteen out of twenty-six. For the years in between, the average has been ten."

"I can't believe this," Helen interjected. "How could this possibly be?"

I continued, forcing myself not to hedge here by softening the information in an effort to protect Helen, "Requests for children not to be placed in your room have gone from three the first year to twenty-two this year, out of a total possible number of 104.

"Staff concern about your teaching has mirrored parent concern. Naturally, the staff concern is focused at the first and third grade levels, those teachers who must place children in your room and those who receive children you taught. I know of three teachers who tried to speak to you directly about their concerns. They have left you feeling rebuffed if not insulted. Other teachers, who don't dare to be open with you, tiptoe through the placement and receiving processes in hopes of not engendering your wrath or your sullen dismissal.

"Finally, I am concerned about your teaching in precisely those ways which parents and other teachers articulate: Your expectations for all children to work independently in an informal, open atmosphere are too high and too universally applied. You tend not to listen to others who have valuable information about the children you teach—those include parents, teachers, the children themselves, and me. You seem to err generally in the direction of not providing enough structure in your program. Finally, you use too much sarcasm with children.

"These are the conclusions I've come to on the basis of the information I've received from others and through direct observation over a period of nine years. I wish I could say they were wide open to change with new, additional information of a different kind from you. Sadly, I doubt it. That's not to say that the door of my mind has slammed completely shut, either. I hope we can talk about what this information means to both of us and what its implications for action are."

"I can't believe you're telling me this," Helen exclaimed, shocked, angry. "How can this possibly be?"

"It's an outrageous situation," I said firmly, meaning it, and indeed I felt very suddenly a deep sadness for the two of us.

We sat in silence for what seemed a long time, though only seconds passed, I think.

Helen sat with a demeanor mixed in disbelief and disgust. I kept reminding myself not to flee, not to silently disappear in mind though remaining present in body. I kept telling myself that sitting there with her was not nothing but *something* to offer, an *action* which was taking courage. Maybe an appropriate action, in fact, given the circumstances.

"Well, sir, you've come to your conclusions. Now what?" Helen said flatly, apparently having decided on sullen dismissal as her way to handle the pain, and me.

Don't back off, I kept saying to myself. Don't start to soften and fudge. "I want you to meet with me in a series of meetings, once a week at this time, to attempt a conversation about this information and its implications for your teaching and my administering. I believe that what you and I have in common is our commitment to children. About that I have no doubt. It is in that commitment, though differently expressed by each of us, that I place my trust and find hope that we might learn together in ways which allow us to better serve children."

I had learned that critical information tends to register in the receiver as, "He's saying I don't care." That meaning is intolerable to live with. Here, at the end, I was trying to say that I was not questioning her caring itself. I was also trying to tell her that I had a commitment to this activity and that the activity had a purpose which I thought was hers as well as mine—to better serve children.

When I finished my little speech, Helen still said nothing, so I got up. She did, too, and left, without a word.

After the First Meeting with Helen

Between this and each successive meeting with Helen, I was meeting with the consultant whom I worked with for several years. When we met, two days after the first meeting with Helen, my first question was, "Now what?"

I'd given Helen the bad news. More than ever, it was clear to me that the negative information I had and didn't share with Helen gave me a feeling of power over her. Now she knew what I knew. We were on equal footing, it seemed.

Of course, we weren't, too. I was the one who initiated the meeting solely because I was the principal. Helen had to come or face consequences. It did not work the other way around. This was a fact which the consultant kept repeating. He kept saying that as long as I didn't face this, my perception would be distorted. I had more power than I *felt*, he said, and he asked me to experience this by my role-playing Helen while he played me.

Still, I was intimidated by Helen, and torn. How far did I want to go with this idea of giving information, negative information, *and then* staying around to discuss it with someone who saw the information very differently? What could really come of it? Was it worth the effort?

The consultant suggested that I might be less anxious if I were more clear about *why* I was involved in this effort. Our discussion of *why* resulted in the following set of questions and answers. The consultant asked the questions, and we sought the answers together:

QUESTION: Why did you give Helen the negative information you had previously withheld?

ANSWER: Because without it, Helen is in the dark, unable to make informed choices.

QUESTION: Why did you want her to have the chance to make informed choices?

ANSWER: Because it is a human right which I believe in (but have tended not to act from).

QUESTION: What is the hoped-for outcome of choosing?

ANSWER: Commitment. It makes commitment possible.

QUESTION: Why is commitment important to you?

ANSWER: Because without commitment, action is hollow, empty, and action characterized in this way is not productive of learning in children.

This format left unstated the central questions of performance:

How do I give and receive negative information in such a way that it is heard and used instead of blocked by denial or distortion?

How do I create conditions which open the possibility for choice and commitment rather than close it off?

Practically speaking, constructing these two sets of questions helped to counteract the impatience in me. My impatience had gotten the better of me in the past, and it was fighting to dominate again—"You've got the bad news, Helen; now shape yourself up or ship out!" When I'm impatient, I just want an end product, like magic, and I feel that as principal, as the authority, I have the right to expect it and get it on command.

The Second Meeting with Helen

I didn't sleep the Thursday night before our second Friday session. When we sat down on Friday, I began, "Helen, have you been thinking about what we talked about last week?"

"Have I been thinking about it?! That's all I've thought about," she exclaimed.

"How do you think we're going to solve this?" I asked.

There was a long silence. I could feel my impatience rising.

I don't know why, but I suddenly heard my own language—I was talking about solving a problem, not about what the problem was or what the information meant—and realized I was closing off the conversation, not opening it! I was desperate for a second before asking myself, "What can this have been like for Helen? Maybe she can't speak her real feelings without my okay."

In retrospect, I realized that in certain situations I needed "legitimization" from others before I could risk saying what I felt because I thought I shouldn't have the feelings in the first place. I needed the consultant to say out loud what I was so afraid of that I couldn't think to say it.

"I'd think, uh . . . you might be furious with me . . ." I "imagined out loud" to Helen, rather clumsily. *I was formulating what I said as I said it, and I was self-conscious. It was very difficult to make myself vulnerable in this way because I risked violating Helen's sense of privacy and incurring her wrath or rejection.*

"I certainly am," she said, hard, cold.

The silence seemed to go on forever. I couldn't think.

"Since you came here," she said, glaring, "you've been out to get me." Again there was a pause. "None of this would have happened to me if you hadn't turned the faculty against me! Just because I dared to speak up!" She continued with a frontal assault, and I had everything I could do to keep from simply taking what she said literally and reacting with a counterpunch.

My counterpunching, reflexive pattern was to hear her accusing me, to feel wrongly accused, and to act with the purpose of correcting her—"Helen, you're saying it's my fault, but it's not. It's your fault."

As a result of acting repeatedly from this pattern for years, I knew I could prevail; I could win the battle of you fault me, then I fault you. But the winning was empty. It didn't produce learning and change, in me or my staff. Here, I kept reminding myself of my new goal—to avoid simply winning; from a more positive perspective, my goal was to promote dialogue and through dialogue, mutual learning.

"So, Helen, this is entirely my fault?" I said, surprising myself. I was imagining out loud for her what I thought she was saying.

"Yes, it is!" Helen was relentless.

So was I. "There's absolutely no question in your mind that I am totally to blame for all that has happened?"

The silence rang on long.

I saw the last two questions I'd just asked Helen as nonliteral or noncontent focused and thereby possibly conducive for learning. I was not listening to her words and tone as if they could be interpreted only as blame of me and then acting from this interpretation by hitting back with righteous counter-blame. To the contrary, I was listening to her words and tone as her mode of explanation, as her way of explaining what had happened between us in our last session and the years before. My questions asked Helen to take full responsibility for her explanation ("It's your fault") and for the tone in which it was offered—as if I were the only possible explanation.

I'd learned that asking another person to take responsibility for their thinking in this way could result in the person having to face the doubt, the questions, the confusion, the ambivalence which is often hidden behind apparent certainty. I'd also found that there is no way I can get directly to that doubt, those questions, that confusion. The other person must offer these vulnerabilities. What I can do, by not getting hooked on listening literally, is ask the other person to make a choice: If Helen says, "Yes, that's the only explanation," she will implicitly be saying that she has no questions, no doubt, no confusion, no ambivalence. This can be a frightening consequence to anticipate yet endure. It's tantamount to publicly declaring yourself "God." If Helen says, "Maybe," or "No," then she's saying there is room for other explanations, and hence there is hope for dialogue and possibly change.

With a burst of sudden words, Helen finally spoke, "How could you keep that from me all this time?! I can't believe that the teachers said those things to you about me . . . Why wouldn't you do me the decency of reporting parent complaints?!"

Though Helen was, in a sense, declaring her vulnerability, I got stuck for a few seconds hearing what she said only as an attack. To myself, I was saying, "Listen, Helen, if you'd listened to the parents and teachers who did go to you, we wouldn't be in this mess right now! You're as defensive and closeminded now as you've always been."

It may sound ridiculous, but after a few anxious seconds like this, I could hear another voice telling me that Helen had just risked revealing new parts of herself—her unanswerable questions, her inability to understand, her vulnerability. Though her tone was outrage and still attacking, her attempts to communicate were in question form: "How could you . . .? Why would you . . .?"

I pressed myself to imagine the inner experience which Helen might be giving expression to in these questions and tone. "She might feel trapped and betrayed as a result of my withholding this information," I told myself. I said something to this effect to Helen, and it seemed to release her outrage and confusion even more.

"It's inconsiderate and irresponsible of you to dump this information on me after all these years. Years! I had no idea that there was such concern about my teaching! I'm a fine teacher. Fine teacher. I don't know what's going on here . . ." Helen's wrath and confusion trailed into silence.

Drawing on my own experience with flailing around as Helen was here, I thought she might be struggling with the fear, the terrible fear of getting close to the fact that she could not make sense of what I told her. The information was too powerful to simply dismiss, yet it could not be made sense of from where she stood in viewing her own teaching; she saw herself as "a fine teacher."

"I wish I hadn't withheld that information, and I think the consequences for you and for me were bad and are terribly painful," I said, beginning to sense a defensiveness in me. "But I don't see myself as irresponsible when viewed from the intention I had at the time—to make a safe, secure setting which would allow for learning, mistaken as I was—"

Helen cut in, "Good intentions are no excuse for bad results."

"I hope you'll apply that thought to your teaching as well as my supervision," I zapped her back and continued, "Had I been more capable that first year of taking up your 'dare to be open' in a more direct way, had I been less intimidated by you—"

Helen cut in again, "You were intimidated by me? How could you say that? You didn't act that way. You just ran over me as if I didn't have a brain in my head."

We went on to share our recollection of that first confrontation. Helen talked about how different the school, community, and principal were before my arrival and, in a way, shared her disappointment in me and my style of leadership. The tone of our conversation began to change from accusatory to reflective until we focused on parent involvement in the school. Helen dismissed my policy of receiving parent requests for transfer and placement as nothing but a slap in the face to teachers.

"Why do you think I take parent requests into account?" I asked, challenging her to hear my side of the issue.

"I don't really care," Helen said flatly.

I was hurt and slapped back, demonstrably angry, "Damn it, Helen, that's exactly what comes through to parents and to me and underlies one of the central complaints about you—that you don't care about what *we* say. You have one god—your expectations of children—and you look only at those expectations to tell you about whether or not you and the children are doing a good job. You refuse to look at and listen to us, and we have important information about these children."

At the time, I felt exhilarated yet vulnerable in expressing my anger to her so directly. The vulnerability resulted from my old idea that a leader is always cool, rational, above the fray. Here, I was hot!

Helen exclaimed, "I said this before and will again. You don't know

anything about the years I've put into this community and its children before
you ever got here with your fancy ideas about what was right about you and
wrong about *us.* There are parents out there right now, if they knew how you
were talking to me . . ."

There were several seconds of quiet.

"How's that?" I asked, with real curiousness. "What am I saying to you?"

*Helen was caught off guard in that way I'd learned to recognize. Here
again, I'd been able not to take her literally and get trapped into automatic
counterattack. I was able to realize that I did not know what meaning she had
made of these discussions and the information I'd revealed, and I was able to
act assertively from my "not knowing" as a resource for inquiry rather than a
liability to hide.*

There was a long silence.

Helen stumbled, "You . . . you're," she hesitated as she came close to
tears, "telling me I'm no good . . . I'm no good . . ." There was a long
pause as she struggled to control. herself. "If you had the nerve, you'd
probably try to get rid of me . . . Isn't that what people want?"

*Clearly, Helen had taken a big risk in making herself vulnerable by
declaring what the information really meant to her, "telling me I'm no
good," "get rid of me." In short, it meant complete rejection. Her hostility,
expressed in a variety of attacks on me to this point, made much more sense
when seen in light of these self-made meanings.*

*Through my experience with times like this, I knew that the act of
revealing herself, of choosing to take a stand behind her own thoughts,
negative as they were, gave her two opportunities which are central to
allowing change: First, she was, for this particular time, giving up the fight to
get the "world" or me to lift from her the burden of feeling the feelings of
utter confusion which were, through the vehicle of parent complaints, the
consequences of her actions. I thought she had to take/feel these feelings as
hers before she could have cause, choice, and commitment to construct new
forms of action which might produce different consequences for children and
for her.*

*Second, the act of taking a stand behind the negative meanings she'd made
of the information allowed her to get new information which could confirm
or disconfirm the sense she'd made.*

*Believe me, I could appreciate her risk. It's awful to declare these negative
thoughts about yourself because, at the time, simply saying the thought out
loud feels like making it come true.*

*In fact, it was not true that everyone wanted me to get rid of her, and it was
not true that everyone, including me, thought she was "no good." For sure,*

there were certain things about her teaching which many of us thought were bad, but that's not the same as saying, "You, Helen, are bad, totally."

I said, "Yes, some of them want to get rid of you." I was straining not to hedge and saying to myself that she had a right to the facts. My instincts were to start to soften the message.

"Some of them want that," I repeated. "But I have not come to that conclusion myself. I have considered it, and I still am considering it, but I have not come to that conclusion right now. And I have not come to the conclusion that you are "no good," though there are things about your teaching which I don't like and others don't like either."

We were both quiet for a moment. Then I continued, "I'd like to suggest that we examine how you work with children and parents, in particular how you set your expectations and hold or fail to hold children to them."

"Well, what if I don't want to do that?" she asked, not belligerently but afraid, almost surprised, that she asked.

"Most importantly, I think you'd be missing a chance to learn," I said, pausing to think for a second about how to declare myself. "I'd also like you to consider a shift in grade level, where your expectations might fit better with older kids. It's a shift to the fifth grade, which is possible. If that doesn't work out, and you can't alter your behavior, I will probably take action against you."

Helen asked, on edge, "Is that a threat?"

"Yes and no. I consider it my responsibility to let you know where I stand."

Helen didn't speak, and in the pause I realized how tired I was. "Helen, do you take it as a threat? And are you tempted to use it against me?" I asked, figuring that at least I'd ask her to put herself on the line.

"No," she said. "I don't think so. But I am having a hard time understanding what's going on here."

"Helen, I'm tired," I said. "It's time to end this. I want you to come again next Friday at this time, and probably for the next three weeks to follow."

She looked—amazed, as if she still didn't think I was serious. "You don't mean it," she stated.

"I do. And please think about whether or not you'll join me in examining why people are dissatisfied with your teaching. I think we have to look at the fact that children are afraid. I can't believe you want to frighten children. You are probably getting results you don't intend. You and I together, I think, can make some headway."

The Third Meeting with Helen

When Helen arrived for our third meeting, she began immediately with a question, "Why do you think I should move to the fifth grade?"

"Helen, I'm not sure you should move. I haven't decided yet. I'm still trying to get information. Do you think I have decided?"

"No, actually . . ." she hesitated. "I don't think you have, for sure. I mean that." Her saying, "I mean that" was somehow new to me—like she knew I'd be skeptical and she wanted to reassure me, wanted me to believe she was genuine. And, in fact, I did, to my surprise.

I began, "I thought of your moving to fifth grade for several reasons. The first is simple luck. There's an opening. Second, all the other fifth grade teachers are more structured in their approach to teaching than you are; your style would provide an option for parents who wanted it. There are parents who want the option. Third, I believe your best friend here is Sharon. She's a fifth grade teacher whose style of teaching I think you respect, as do I. The two of you might help one another."

She said, "I don't even know what I'd do with fifth graders. . . ." Her voice trailed off into silent thought.

I replied, "Fifth grade kids are able to do a lot more independent work, and you encourage kids to work independently." As I continued giving this pep talk, I realized that though I believed what I said, I'd missed the point.

Without conscious thought, I'd automatically assumed that Helen's statement of concern about never having worked with fifth graders was a call for support, for reassurance that she could handle it. So, I jumped right in with my pep talk, rescuing her from her own uncertainties.

I'd learned to mistrust my tendency to rescue others from their own uncertainties; though, as indicated here, my tendency was still strong. My own efforts to learn taught me that uncertainties, though they feel like a plague, can be the seeds which, with careful care, grow into new trust and confidence.

I wanted Helen to be able to talk out her uncertainties in this setting where she might search her way through them and get some new perspectives. I did not want my responses to contribute to her covering them over or denying that they existed. The negative results could be that the uncertainties would simply stay as knots of confusion inside her and be acted out when she was alone with children.

Fortunately, there was a rather long pause which gave me time to recover.

"Helen, maybe you were saying that you were pretty concerned about such a move. . . ."

Interrupting me, she spoke, "Yes, I am. . . . I have no experience with older children, and, I don't know . . . it would be like starting all over again. . . ." Her voice trailed off and her eyes began to fill with tears.

I had no idea what would happen next. Several seconds of silence passed.

Apparently on a new course, Helen began, "I was awfully upset after that last meeting, and I don't think I can take another like it." There began to be an edge of anger in her voice.

"Don't misunderstand me, though," she went on, "I am terribly hurt. It seems there's been a conspiracy of silence against me. I have thought of nothing for weeks but the awful things which you have said to me. . . ." She paused for some seconds, then said, "But I can see that you are trying to be honest with me."

I was conscious of a sigh breaking from me, as if I'd been holding my breath. I felt understood by and genuinely warm toward Helen for the first time in these meetings.

Helen went on, "I don't know. I don't think I can go further with this . . . at least right now. . . ."

If I hadn't been through moments like this myself, I doubt if I would have been able to feel compassion for Helen here. I might have thought, "She's trying to pull my chain. Give me the tears and helplessness treatment."

But instead, I thought, "She's divided inside about whether or not to continue." So I asked if this were true.

Helen sat quietly, nodded yes, once again seemingly close to tears.

Several seconds passed.

"Do I really have a choice about moving to the fifth grade?" she asked.

She had pushed me right to the wall. I hesitated and then took the plunge.

"Yes, you have choice. And so do I. Let me see if I can tell you where I stand. If you stay in the second grade, I'll have to begin formally documenting a case for your removal, though at the same time I will continue to try to work with you to improve the situation. If you choose to move to grade five, I'll agree. But I'll have a clear expectation about seeing more rigorous, structured programs for certain children, more listening and taking into account information about children offered by others, and less reliance on sarcasm in your relations with children, and I would hope, faculty. I've tried to say that the heart of this matter *might* be corrected with a move in grade level. I hope so, but I have my doubts."

Helen spoke. "I think I'd like to think about this some more. Can we stop for today?"

I was again disappointed that she asked.

"Okay," I said. "But I want you to schedule two more of these Friday meetings at this same time."

"*Two* more," she said, disgruntled.

"Yes. Two more. Next time, before we discuss moving to fifth grade, I want to discuss further the possibility of the two of us examining this second grade situation some more."

After the Third Meeting with Helen

Right after we ended, I had an awful attack of anxiety. Was I making a fool of myself? I traced the anxiety back to how vulnerable I felt now that I had gone even further in giving Helen information, this time about exactly where I stood. I had given her information about both what I would and would not do and the consequences to her of the various alternatives. And by not trying to force her to stay and talk, I hoped I'd given her a message in action that I'd respect *her* choices.

Still, my feelings called me back to old forms of behavior: be in control, don't be vulnerable, don't let feelings get into your work. I started feeling pretty sorry for myself. It wasn't until later that evening that I was able to regain some perspective.

As I see it, how I feel about myself depends on how I think about my responsibility here. If I think according to some general definition of good leadership, then I evaluate myself according to this definition—be in control, don't be vulnerable, keep feelings out. Measuring what I did with Helen against the yardstick of these definitions, I come out looking like a fool and feeling punk.

Yet, if I think differently, from a different definition of what is possible in leadership, emphasizing that I care by being willing to confront, instead of protect; by offering real choice; by giving and receiving information, positive and negative; by trying to promote dialogue and through it mutual commitment; and by risking being vulnerable, then, when I look at what I did with Helen, I feel sometimes great, other times not half bad.

When I met with the consultant and reviewed the third session, we focused on two ideas: one, that there is much more to Helen than what I see in the classroom and school and two, a distinction between evaluation and supervision.

First, to me there may be no rhyme nor reason for how Helen treats kids, no apparently valid explanations, but they are there. And, they have to be gotten to if lasting change is to occur. And, they have to be gotten to by *her.* In other words, her experience which leads her to teach as she does must be the subject matter of a self-conducted inquiry which I can take part in, if she is willing, but I can't "pull it off," force it to happen. It's got to be two-way, not one-way.

I might be tempted to take bright ideas which I've come to through *my* experience in life, like light bulbs, and hand them over to Helen on the assumption that all she would have to do is screw the bulbs into the right socket and they would light her up! Think of the time it would save, her not having to go through what I did to come to my conclusions. She could simply put them right to work, lighting up children's lives.

Unfortunately, as I had found in the past, and the consultant confirmed, the bulbs don't often light up. My good advice makes no sense to someone else. Or, I've found, if it makes sense in words, it comes out cockeyed in action. Sometimes I've given a teacher advice about how to handle a classroom situation, assumed that the teacher understood the advice, and then, when I saw what the teacher did, found that I did not recognize my advice (or wished I hadn't).

In short, I had to keep from jumping out of impatience into quick-and-easy advice or solutions and try to keep inventing ways to "imagine out loud" and "get myself on the map" in an effort to provide solutions through dialogue—painful, slow, and difficult as this was.

Second, in this session with the consultant he asked, "What if Helen is willing to look at her teaching with you—and that would be a big risk for her—how will you act as a supervisor with her?" We came back to the idea of combining supervision and evaluation. He had a useful view on this combination, specifically relating to my efforts with Helen.

So far in my encounters with Helen, his thinking went, I had acted mostly as evaluator and administrator. As evaluator, I had judged Helen's performance against external criteria for performance, mine and the community's, found her wanting, and delivered the bad news. As administrator, I exercised my legitimate authority in setting up a structure (the *series* of meetings) for sharing this information and for trying to make supervision possible.

As supervisor, I judge Helen not just by external criteria but by the internal criteria of where Helen *is now* as opposed to where she *was* in her efforts to learn. As yet, I hadn't had the chance to supervise, though I'd invited Helen to join me in trying to learn. If she gave me the chance to supervise, what skills would I have to use?

The Fourth Meeting with Helen

Helen had hardly seated herself for our fourth session before she began to speak. What she said again brought home to me the vast distances between her experience, her way of seeing things, and mine.

"You don't see that forcing everyone to do the same work," Helen began, "is exactly the wrong thing to do! Because a few children are afraid of working on their own and can't keep busy, you want me to make everyone do the same thing, like little robots. If anything, the workbook mentality of most teachers does more harm to children than my individualized approach. You're criticizing me because the 'back-to-basics' people are pressuring you." She stopped and waited for a reply.

"Maybe I've implied that you should totally stop individualizing your program and make all children do the same work," I offered, "but I haven't meant to . . ."

I hadn't finished when Helen began again. "I teach the 'basics' better than most teachers. I did ten years ago, and I still do today! Why can't the parents who want a more individualized approach have me as an alternative? You're fond of touting the importance of alternatives," she turned the word with sarcasm.

"I am in favor of alternatives," I said flatly. "As I said the last time we met, I think you would present an alternative at the fifth grade level."

"Why not at the second grade level?" Helen continued on with the attack, using the sarcastic tone she knew I did not like her using with children, or on me.

"Because I'm troubled about what happens between you and second graders," I said, obviously angry.

Helen burst out, "You . . ." She faltered before finding words, "You're *troubled* about how I teach second graders, are you? Well, I'm *troubled* about how you discipline children. You don't!" She seemed to be blatantly baiting me with sarcastic turns on my word *troubled*.

She continued, "When I send a child to the office, I want him punished. I wouldn't send him if he didn't deserve it. You never back me up. And there are other teachers who feel this way, too."

I knew well that Jane felt this way, so I was shaken by the content of what Helen said, apart from her tone, which angered me. I made a big decision to step into Helen's criticism for the purpose of opening to it rather than trying to stop her attack with a counterargument.

Speaking quite deliberately at first, because I was afraid, I began, "Last year another teacher complained about how I discipline. It shook me then, as you do now, because I've been quite satisifed with my discipline. To me it's important to talk with kids in a nonthreatening way so I can help them get to the causes of their misbehavior, instead of reacting with punishment to the symptoms, to the misbehavior itself."

As I talked, I felt more sure of myself. I was contending with two silent issues as I spoke. First, my hope in opening to Helen's criticism was to avoid getting hooked on the blunt, attacking tone and manner of her criticism, as I had years before. Then, all my attention was wasted on looking at how she "confronted" me. For several years I was preoccupied with the manner of her confrontation rather than the content. I did not want to repeat my old pattern, but not doing so was terribly difficult because the alternative was to make myself vulnerable.

Second, in trying to respond to the content of Helen's criticism, in making myself vulnerable to it, I felt as if I were losing control, simply submitting to her tactics of drawing me away from the real issue—her teaching. In fact, a part of me was saying, "You're doing just what she wants—focusing on your work as administrator and thereby avoiding an examination of her teaching." In short, I was struggling with a tendency to call myself a stupid weakling for apparently giving up control.

I had paused for a few seconds after telling Helen of my hope to get to causes rather then react to symptoms of misbehavior, and she spoke, breaking the silence. But I cut her off, telling her I wanted to finish.

"I've been meeting my own expectations for performance in this area of disciplining children, but not yours and not those of another experienced teacher . . ." I paused again, searching for what to make of this criticism. "You and others have said this to me before, that I don't punish children enough, and I've simply argued with you, trying to get you to see my view and buy it. . . . What I never did do with the whole staff is open up the question of a school policy toward discipline . . . I just made my policy the whole school's policy." I was at once excited by my insight and feeling very vulnerable, partly because Helen was giving me a blank look.

I went on, "If I were to—" I stopped suddenly, switching direction. I addressed Helen, "What would you do if you were me, and you'd just gotten information from two of your experienced teachers that they did not think you were serving either their needs or those of children in the way you gave discipline, but you liked the way you handled discipline? it seemed like the best way to you . . ."

My hope here was to find a way to break the pattern of Helen-attacks-and-Lew-responds. Would Helen consciously see the game we were playing? What I had asked her to do—look at her relationship with kids—she had asked me to do relative to how I disciplined, and I'd nibbled at the bait. Now I was trying to turn the request for inquiring back to her.

"I don't know," Helen said, backing away.

"Come on," I urged her. "Don't back out now," and I almost added in laughter, "I dare you."

"It's your job," Helen said. "And you're trying to trap me somehow."

"Not exactly, I'm not trying to hurt you, Helen," I replied. "Isn't this situation of your complaining about how I discipline similar to my complaining about how you teach? Each of us thinks we are doing the best for kids, yet other people are challenging what we do, questioning it. Each of us is asking the other to stop defending *why* we do what we do and examine *how* we are doing it, and perhaps change."

There was a long pause before Helen spoke, surprising me. "I'm afraid the two situations are similar," she said.

There was a long pause. I didn't know where we were going from here.

"So what *is* the problem with children being afraid?" Helen asked, saddened, but apparently making a choice and tentative commitment to look at her teaching with me.

Her question allowed me to try to use supervision skills which to this point in our conversation were not appropriate because they work only if there's mutual commitment built on at least a modicum of trust measured in both parties' willingness to make themselves vulnerable.

"I think the thing to do," I began, "would be to look at a particular child, say, Henry." Henry was a child we'd had to talk briefly about in the past because Helen had difficulty with him not doing his work, and his parents had asked for him to be transferred to another room—something I couldn't do.

"When it comes to the end of a writing period and Henry has again not done his work, what goes through your mind?" I asked Helen.

"Goes through my mind?" she said, puzzled.

"Yes. Do you recall—?" I stopped and changed direction. "The idea here is that you've got reasons for treating him as you do. We have to look at those reasons if we're going to try to understand what you do."

I was having a tough time, but Helen helped out by speaking her thoughts about Henry.

"He makes me furious. I've gone out of my way for him, but he doesn't work."

"Concretely, what does he do that makes you so angry?" I asked.

"He doesn't work."

"For example?"

"He horses around and doesn't get his work done!"

"How come he horses around? Do you think—?"

"Because he's lazy. He doesn't want to do his work," Helen stated, assertively. This set of exchanges was tense but not testy.

I paused before asking, "How do you know?" I couldn't figure out how to ask this question without raising defensiveness.

"It's obvious, isn't it?" Helen snapped. "Why else would he horse around all the time?" Helen's testiness was less strident than earlier. She was asking questions, possibly open to puzzling. Still, I wondered if she heard me as saying that she was to blame, the sole cause of Henry's difficulties; I didn't think this, but I could see how she might think I did.

I changed course a bit. "What do you do when he doesn't have his work done?"

Helen was cautious and afraid. "I do what you say I shouldn't do. I get sarcastic."

There was an uncomfortably long pause while I struggled to imagine what hope or assumption might lay under her use of sarcasm.

"What you are trying to do, though," I spoke slowly, trying to find words for an insight, ". . . are you attempting to motivate Henry? Might that be . . . what you're after?" I asked this uncertainly, but I was quite pleased.

In the past, inappropriate behavior, like sarcasm with children, has precipitated such an immediate "No, stop that" reaction in me that I simply pointed it out, condemned it, and then repeated pointing-and-condemning even though I failed to get results. Teachers made sure they weren't sarcastic when I was around; for example, but when I wasn't . . . And worse, teachers saw me as treating them exactly as I'd told them not to treat children, which undermined their confidence in my ability to be useful. They saw me as just "mouthing off."

Here, in saying ". . . aren't you attempting to motivate Henry?" I had broken out of my old pattern of saying, "That's wrong, right it!" It seems that this kind of "That's wrong, right it" statement often gets heard by teachers as, "You don't care, because if you did, then you wouldn't treat children this way." Understandably, their reaction is to fight back rather than examine and alter their behavior, even though they might wish to.

Here, with Helen, I was able to imagine out loud the hope (to motivate) which might be behind her inappropriate sarcastic behavior. This emphasis on her hope rather than her behavior allowed me to highlight the fact that Helen cared about Henry, instead of highlighting the fact that she had terribly limited ways of showing that care.

I think this different emphasis, on confirming her caring, makes it more possible for Helen to stop holding on to and defending the particular act of sarcasm, for example, and open to the possibility of examining its negative consequences and eventually, perhaps, giving it up.

When I asked Helen if she weren't trying to motivate Henry through sarcasm, she was obviously caught off guard. "Well, yes, . . . that's what I want. . . ." She was searching for words. "I want to spur him to work. . . ." Her voice trailed off, but I could sense her mind working, puzzling.

"But it doesn't work with Henry, the sarcasm. He still doesn't want to come to school."

"That's true," Helen agreed. "But if he'd just settle down . . . and his parents could help with that. They are too lax with him."

"Maybe you're right about the parents," I said, purposefully avoiding the fruitless debate I could see ahead.

There was a long pause before I ventured alternative ways of looking at Henry, "I was wondering, though, maybe Henry fools around not because he's lazy but because he doesn't know what he's supposed to do or he's afraid to do it, or . . ."

"But the tasks I lay out are explained in written directions," Helen said.

I asked, "What's puzzling is why he wouldn't get it, because others do—"

Helen interrupted, "What would you have me do, single him out more than I already do?"

"More of that kind of special treatment wouldn't be good; it would be no gift to him . . .?" I asked.

"That's correct," Helen said. "The others would single him out then, and make fun because he's slow."

"And in addition," I was thinking out loud, testing my idea of the positive hopes which might lie behind what I saw as negative actions, "it would be like making it easy on him and contributing to making him soft—"

Helen was breaking in, "Yes, that's right."

I went on, "And he has to learn to read directions himself . . ."

Helen cut in again, excited, "Or where will he be when he's an adult? He can't expect people to go out of their way for him. He's got to develop independence, to be able to take care of himself."

I recognized Helen's excitement. It comes from feeling heard, from being known and respected for your effort and positive hopes, as separate from the outcome of that effort or hope. I was excited, too, because Helen was becoming a real person to me as I could see her positive hopes behind the very actions which I found inappropriate. I still found those actions inappropriate. I wasn't sanctioning sarcastic behavior. But I did want to bring to light and sanction her thinking, not because I thought that would make her feel more jusitifed in her behavior but because it would allow her to get some distance on her thinking and open it to questioning.

As simpleminded as it sounds, I did something I'd never done with Helen; I asked if she'd like coffee or tea, and when she said, "Yes," I went to another part of my office to make it.

As I was getting water for the coffee, Helen began to speak, "What if Henry is afraid . . . or, what was it you said?" She was searching. "You were suggesting that it's not that he doesn't want to work. You were saying that maybe he does want to work but doesn't know how . . . for some reason?" She was very deliberate, apparently in an attempt to check with me about what I'd said earlier.

Here, it seemed to me, Helen was reaching out for the first time to take in a different idea which I had offered. She was, however tentatively, asserting her capacity and right to change her ideas. I think I enabled this act through my efforts to imagine out loud the inner world of her thought and feeling.

Helen had asked if she understood what I said earlier—that perhaps Henry was not lazy but afraid—and I confirmed her understanding. "Yes, you've got the gist of my thought."

Helen began, "I haven't thought about it that way. I just thought . . . I guess I never really thought . . ." Her voice trailed off. "Actually, I like the boy; he's got such vigor. It's just that he doesn't apply himself . . ." She paused, apparently saddened. "Do you have something in mind that you want me to do?" she asked me.

"Not right off the top of my head," I replied, wishing I had a neat solution, pleased that I did not get seduced into thinking that I ought to have one or what good was I, anyway!

I queried, "When you work with him individually, what . . .?"

"I've gone out of my way to try to speak with him about applying himself more diligently, but I get nowhere," Helen said.

The phrase "applying himself more diligently" was a red flag to me, but I reminded myself not to get hooked on her abstract description of what she did. "Seek the concrete; find out what she actually said to the boy," I told myself.

I suggested, "Maybe if we looked at a specific time when you talked with him individually and tried to come up with some different approaches?" I was on the right track but faltered, "I was thinking that today you and I have found we can talk differently together. I think there's hope for you and me in this, and there might be, too, for learning from what you and I have done and extending it to how you might talk with Henry—"

I went too fast here, as I do when I'm tired. Helen stepped in, saying, "Oh, I don't know what I'd say to him."

I surprised myself by avoiding cheap reassurance; instead, I stayed with imagining out loud the point of view from which she might be speaking.

"You're not sure how you'd keep from getting angry and disapproving, caught in the same kind of trap you always get into with him?" I asked. "Yes, . . ." Helen said, again surprised. "How did you know?"

I took the chance to tell her about my own learning and how I'd found it helpful in talking with her today. We agreed that we would meet again the next week and settle the question of moving to the fifth grade, as well as talk about how she might work differently with Henry.

We agreed, but I sensed her uncertainty.

After the Fourth Meeting with Helen

Helen sent me a note before our fifth meeting: "We need not meet again. I have decided to move to the fifth grade." I was disappointed to get the note because I hoped Helen might be ready to make a commitment to working with me in supervision; my immediate reaction was, "Oh, damn it, I thought we'd gotten someplace!"

But, soon after, when I reviewed the past four meetings, I reconfirmed my feeling that I'd seen movement from self-protective monologue to dialogue in which each of us "dared to open." Surely, Helen could close down and deny the tentative commitment to learning which she seemed to risk in the fourth session. But, I decided not to allow her that choice without my giving her more information because, I reasoned, she (like Henry) might be backing away now, not because she didn't want to learn but because she was afraid.

I sent Helen a note: "We do need to meet again to discuss the move."

She caught me in the hall after I put the note in her mailbox.

"Lew," she said, her face hard and fixed, "I don't think it is necessary for us to meet again."

"It is," I said flatly, though tempted to make a nervous joke.

"I could go to the union," she said slowly, "and file a grievance for harrassment."

My automatic, "Oh damn . . ." faded into a long sigh, and feeling sorry for myself, silently I exclaimed, "All this work, and it comes to this!" Still, I lifted my arm, pointing for Helen (and for me) to go into an empty room nearby. I had no idea what I was going to say.

"Helen, I don't think you really want to go to the union. I think you would rather work in supervision with me, but you seem afraid, naturally enough. I hope you will not act from your fear and go to the union, but challenge it by meeting with me.

"I hope you'll show up at the regular time tomorrow." With that, I left.

As I walked to my office, I found myself thinking that Helen had called my bluff, or at least that's the way I read it, and I returned the call and raised. I waited anxiously to see what she would do.

The Fifth Meeting with Helen

Helen came. I was surprised at how glad I was to see her, but she didn't give me much time to feel good.

"I'll tell you what this is like. It is humiliating. You are singling me out, as you would have me do with Henry, and shaming me in front of my colleagues."

I felt a twinge of guilt, but that's all. I was getting quite good at not taking Helen's pain as my personal responsibility.

"I'm sure this has been and will be quite painful. My hope, and perhaps yours, is that what will come of it is more learning for children. That's what you and I are here for, what we're committed to, and the central reason for our going through this gut-wrenching process.

"Helen, I'd like to follow up on our last discussion of Henry, where we were looking at your use of sarcasm, and I'd like to leave here today with a plan for your moving to fifth grade, a plan which will have the result of your changing aspects of your teaching we've discussed in these meetings."

"You don't trust me to change on my own, do you?" Helen stated, a bit sarcastically. She knew well that I valued "learning on your own."

"No, I don't, at least not entirely. But I don't see that as a negative comment on you so much as a statement of my belief that change is very difficult and necessitates regular support. Actually, what I don't trust in you is your ability to provide yourself with the necessary support. I don't see how you could trust yourself in this way, given your experience in this school as an isolate and loner."

We sat quietly for several seconds before Helen's eyes began to tear.

"No one's taken the time with me before . . ." she said, sadly.

We sat in a long silence. I was sad myself.

Helen began, "You're right, I don't trust myself to get help. I've always thought it unprofessional, an admission of incompetence."

She continued, "When I was making up my mind to move to the fifth grade—you will allow the move, won't you?"

"Yes."

"When making up my mind, I thought a great deal about what you've said during these meetings, and I do want to do something about my teaching. In fact, I've already begun." She stopped, waited.

"I'm curious," I said, "How have you begun?"

She described at length how she occasionally found herself observing her children differently, Henry, for example. She said she could see that Henry's and other children's horsing around might be seen as "unproductive" or "wasting time," interpretations which she'd tended to find unthinkable in the past; that is, even though the horsing around bothered her, she tended to allow it and defined it in educational terms as "creative play" or "learning to express themselves."

She had begun to think that perhaps some of the children were wild not because they did not want to work or because they needed to learn to express themselves, but because she was not providing an appropriate set of structures which would allow them to work productively, even creatively. She said that she could and was going further in the direction of giving certain students more rigorous programs of study while at the same time allowing other students to keep their leeway.

Already, she'd found a problem which she'd anticipated—some students made fun of others whom she required to work according to a tighter program. Helen found this intolerable and voiced a need for help in how to handle such situations.

She said she was beginning to recognize how often she was sarcastic with children, much more than she'd known. As yet, she was unable to act otherwise, but recognition seemed to me to be the first and necessary step to possible change, and I told her so.

We worked out a two-part plan for the remainder of the year which would enable a successful move to the fifth grade. She would meet with me once a month after I visited her classroom, and we would continue working on the areas in her teaching and my administering which we'd begun to discuss. At my prompting, we agreed to meet together with Helen's friend Sharon and discuss with Sharon the possibility of her working with Helen. Sharon had a marvelous way of combining "open classroom" and "traditional" methodologies. Helen and I agreed that Sharon presented a model for the teaching-learning process which was worth trying to understand and approximate in action.

Our lengthy but satisfying session ended with Helen telling me that she had not known what my expectations for her performance were before this series of meetings. She thought it would be a good idea if I made my expectations more clear to everyone, not just her. I agreed and told her that this series of meetings had forced me to be more clear about my expectations than I had ever been before. In this way, she had again contributed to my learning.

After the Fifth Meeting with Helen

Now, I realize that the kind of change reported by Helen in this final session can be so much pap. It wasn't though, and I didn't think it was at the time. I've seen Helen teach since this meeting, and she's changing, intelligently, at that! Other members of the faculty report changes in Helen which confirm my perception.

A week or so after that fifth meeting, I decided to affirm my commitment to continuing to work with Helen by visiting her after school and asking if she'd continue the conversation about Henry. Mistrust built up over years runs very deep, right?

Was I surprised by Helen's reception? When I asked about continuing our look at Henry, she said, "I thought you'd never ask," making a joke, yet! She told me she had been trying to work individually with Henry, but after hearing her describe the work, it seemed to me that she lacked the internal perspective and skill to work more successfully with him. She seemed torn between reaching out to help him and feeling that this very act did him a disservice. That internal conflict came out as impatience and anger with his slowness. We spent a few minutes trying to clarify the internal conflict she felt and imagining ways of working differently with Henry.

This conflict is not Helen's only problem, and even it is not resolved, but that afternoon I think she had another experience of finding that she could expose herself and learn and come away with hope rather than humiliation. From my attempts to learn I found how necessary it was to go through repetition upon repetition of this pattern before I could break through years of mistrust which kept me hidden.

Conclusion

So, to try to conclude this lengthy tale, the word got out about my work with Helen. The Assistant Superintendent has a problem with one of his central office people, and he wants to know how I faced Helen.

I plan to meet with him, though I fear he's in for a disappointment. Knowing him, he may want a short do-it-yourself course, the cream off the top, if you know what I mean—six easy steps you can take to confront that staff person who intimidates you.

Maybe I'm cynical about this colleague, and others. If so, it comes out of a kind of loneliness right now. As I've risked revealing my fears to myself and others and experimented with changing my leadership, I've come into a loneliness quite different from that I felt when I was isolated from my staff and other colleagues during my first few years on this job.

Before, I was lonely because of lack of contact with others, for a chance to be, as I call it, given sanction to be a human being in this job; I was incomplete, partial, full of feelings and thoughts which for some reason I assumed a leader could not have and still be an effective leader. I fell prey to taking things literally, personally, to seeing myself as the center and cause of what other people were thinking and doing. I felt an all-encompassing responsibility which was very heady. I saw myself as very needed. Things could not go on without me. But, fortunately, I say in hindsight, I tired of the weight of this kind of responsibility.

As I think back, I see the kernel of my strength in my ability to admit to myself that the skills I needed for the future I did not have at the time, even though I was running a good school, as they say, and would have continued to do so. It was difficult to open the door to my inner life and that of others, but doing so opened the door to many more doors I've opened since. As I've opened them, I've found what it is like to have thoughts of my own, thoughts which aren't governed by the demands of being liked, being right, being in control, being invulnerable.

Again, of course, I'm saying this with the benefit of majestic hindsight. There's no way I could have known that my thinking was formed by those underlying dictates—be liked, be right, be in control, be invulnerable. I was above being controlled by such juvenile tendencies. I was, in my own mind, only interested in having the respect of the people I worked with, and getting the job done. But I was fooling myself.

Now that I have some thoughts of my own, well, there's a different kind of loneliness, as I was saying before. I thought growth would do away with pain, like this loneliness. It seems to come when I ask, "Did I do the right thing?" and realize that I'm the one who has to answer my own question.

Don't get me wrong. At the same time, I like to answer my own question. There's such a feeling of potency in having an internal reference point which allows me to self-reward and self-correct my own action as a leader. What I'm talking about is a set of criteria, really, which differ from those I paid homage to without knowing it—the gods of being liked, being right, being in control, being invulnerable. These gods seem to underlie my tendency to set up win-lose interactions, to overprotect by withholding information, to keep feelings out of professional matters.

This old system of thought and action had me placing more trust in the expectations which others had for me as a leader than in my own expectations for myself. Of course, a ready-made *me*, all formed with expectations of my own for leadership, did not already exist someplace just waiting to be found. I had to discover my inner life and actively build a new trust in who I actually was, in a voice of my own, as person and professional.

13 | Commentary on Lew's Case

In the case of Lew, we see a leader trying to restructure his leadership style so that it corresponds with his reconstructed definition of himself. He has gone through the learning phases discussed in the rest of the book and is able to call upon his experience to help another learn. He also has an organized framework with which to think about what he does, change what he does, and plan for how he is going to make progress toward his emerging redefinition of leadership. These represent an enormous accomplishment.

With respect to the learning process, Lew is graphic about the discrepancies he discovered in his leadership and about how he started upon his own learning. We sense that Lew has experienced the same sort of things Tom, Paul, and Steve describe as they examined their practice. Lew's capacity to translate his learning into action shows that he spent a significant period of time, like Joe, developing skills that enable him to reach out to another person. We also see Lew go further than the others and put into action his learning about himself and others in ways that use his position as a leader to create the conditions for learning.

We will now examine in detail how Lew Takes New Action with Helen, and then we will look at the definition of leadership which appears to be emerging for Lew.

162

Lew Takes New Action

The case just presented shows a leader Taking New Action. Looking only at Lew's actions, what he does with Helen could be considered cruel. He confronts her a number of times, gives her extremely negative information, insists she join with him in a series of meetings, and even challenges her intent to go the union with a grievance about him.

Yet, as a result of Lew's behavior, Helen appears to experience consequences which are unexpected from the perspective that Lew's actions are cruel. The consequences to Helen of Lew's actions include the following:

Helen recognizes that there is a problem concerning her teaching.

Helen confronts the fact that she cannot make sense of the information from Lew that she is not perceived as a good teacher.

Helen brings into the exchange between them a large range of her own sense-making processes, including rage, humiliation, and fear.

Helen makes a choice about whether or not to inquire into the discrepancy between her own view of teaching and that of others.

Helen recognizes and explores, within a concrete situation, some of her assumptions about motivating and preparing children.

Helen entertains the possibility of a different set of assumptions regarding the motivation and preparation of children.

Helen begins, in short, to alter her perceptions and behavior.

This list of consequences parallels what we have called learning. We call Lew's action "new" because it creates the conditions not for competition but for learning. Helen is helped to confront discrepancies, choose to inquire into them, explore her thoughts, feelings, and assumptions, entertain alternative assumptions, and begin to change. This is a remarkable set of outcomes.

Looking not only at outcomes but also at Lew, we see that his actions are new in terms of his assumption of personal responsibility for his actions and the assumptions on which they are based. Where before he did not recognize the assumptions governing his behavior and tended to blame others, now he accepts responsibility both for the consequences of his new assumptions and for the old ones (as when he becomes angry with Helen). Because he now holds assumptions which he has chosen and to which he feels commitment, it appears he can hold them both more firmly and tentatively than he did his old assumptions about which, at one level, he was sure he was right and, at deeper levels, felt insecure.

Taking Personal Responsibility

One of the results of the personal learning involved in examining practice is that one learns to take responsibility for one's assumptions. One learns to know and accept one's limits as a person. We see what taking personal responsibility can look like when we view Lew's behavior in "putting himself on the map."

Lew takes personal responsibility by sharing with Helen a range of information including his data, his interpretations of that data, and the action he plans to take as a result of his interpretations. He shares with Helen:

information about his feelings and thoughts about her in the past

information about his feelings and thoughts about her in the moment

information about her past performance gathered from himself, parents and others

information about the interpretations or conclusions he has come to on the basis of information about her past performance

information about the action he intends to take

In their first meeting Lew clearly articulates to Helen the ways in which he thinks he was responsible for the problem between them. He not only volunteers that information at the beginning of the meeting, but, more impressively, he continues to accept responsibility for his part even when she attacks him:

Helen spoke immediately, "I've always thought you were biased against me because of that incident."

"I know," I replied, "and you have been right about my bias."

Lew's taking responsibility for his part assumes a different form when he "accompanies" Helen in her pain at his news of parental requests:

Helen sat with a demeanor mixed in disbelief and disgust. I kept reminding myself not to flee, not to silently disappear in mind, though remaining present in body. I kept telling myself that sitting there with her was not nothing but *something* to offer, an *action* which was taking courage. Maybe an appropriate action, in fact, given the circumstances.

In the second meeting, when Helen attacks Lew—bringing up the very feelings associated with their past confrontation that she had earlier dismissed as silly—he manages to avoid fighting back and instead asks Helen to take some responsibility for her absolutist definition of the problem.

When Helen dismisses with a snippy remark Lew's statement of his intent to make the school a "safe, secure setting," he allows himself a sharp retort. Then he gets really angry and feels both exhilarated and vulnerable in exposing his anger. His taking responsibility for his feelings begins at this point to have obvious consequences for the other person as Helen risks revealing what Lew's statement means to her:

"You . . . you're," she hesitated as she came close to tears, "telling me I'm no good . . . I'm no good." There was a long pause as she struggled to control herself. "If you had the nerve, you'd probably try to get rid of me . . . Isn't that what people want?"

After Helen's remark, Lew squarely states where he stands:

"Some of them want that," I repeated. "But I have not come to that conclusion myself. I have considered it and am still considering it, but I have not come to that conclusion right now. And I have not come to the conclusion that you are 'no good,' though there are things about your teaching which I don't like, and others don't like either."

In the third meeting, Helen asks whether she really has a choice about moving to the fifth grade. This pushes Lew to be as explicit as he can about his position and his expectations. His directness and lack of equivocation are impressive and may play a part in allowing Helen to request that they end the session so she can have time to think.

After the meeting, Lew experiences anxiety. His clarity with Helen has further exposed him. He has given her the information as to where he stands and he feels extraordinarily vulnerable. He knows he cannot later fall back on equivocation and ambiguity since he has been unequivocal and unambiguous in stating his position.

In the fourth meeting Lew shares his feelings a number of times, most notably when he acknowledges the criticisms about his discipline, indicating that the criticisms disturb him. His acknowledging the apparent validity of her criticisms appears to help her come to the point of acknowledging the similarities between their situations.

Finally and paradoxically Lew takes personal responsibility by *not* taking responsibility for Helen's feelings. In the first meeting with Helen when she sullenly dismisses him, Lew says to himself:

"Don't back off," I kept saying to myself. "Don't start to soften and fudge."

He resists his inclination to step in and attempt to soften her pain by retreating from what he has said. Yet at the same time he offers her a statement about her commitment to children as a way to assert that he does not question her caring.

In the fourth meeting as we have seen, Lew does not take responsibility for Helen's feelings when she sarcastically criticizes his disciplining of children. Instead of joining her in tone and engaging in the same behavior, he accepts the issue she raises but not the tone she uses, confirms her by acknowledging that the previous year another teacher has also criticized his disciplining methods, and invites her to join him in examining them.

In the fifth meeting when Helen attacks Lew, he explicitly sums up the skill:

I felt a twinge of guilt but that's all. I was getting quite good at not taking Helen's pain as my personal responsibility.

Recognizing the Other Person

Another set of skills which are productive of learning instead of competition result both from the personal learning of Examining Practice and also from the more interpersonal learning which we have labeled Translation. These are the skills Lew calls "listening nonliterally" and "imagining out loud." What he is describing is the capacity to reach out to another person in ways that "recognize" them.

At a number of critical points in the case, Lew is able to reach out and listen to Helen not in terms of what she is actually saying but from the perspective of what might lie behind the assertion. Then he tests what he thinks he hears by articulating it for her to confirm or disconfirm.

During the second meeting, Helen is at first silent when Lew expects her to speak about the situation. He decides to imagine out loud what she might be feeling as a way to legitimize her feelings and says,

"I'd think, uh . . . you might be furious with me . . ."

This releases Helen to speak her outrage. When she focuses the problem on him, blaming him, he again imagines out loud.

"So, Helen, this is entirely my fault? . . . There's absolutely no question in your mind that I am totally to blame for all that has happened?"

She confirms that it is not entirely his fault by shifting the dialogue to the fact that he withheld information. When he responds, by imagining out loud that Helen's attacks might come from her feeling trapped and betrayed by his withholding information, she confirms that this is true by becoming even angrier.

In the third meeting, Lew imagines out loud when he says, "Helen, maybe you were saying that you were pretty concerned about such a move . . .," and again when he imagines that she is divided about whether to continue working with him.

Lew's most dramatic successes in listening nonliterally come when he recognizes and tentatively articulates what might be Helen's hopes for motivating children.

"What you are trying to do, though . . . are you attempting to motivate Henry? Might that be . . . what you're after?"

"And in addition," I was thinking out loud testing my idea of the positive hopes which might lie behind what I saw as negative actions, 'it would be like making it easy on him, and contributing to making him soft . . .'"

"And he has to learn to read directions himself . . ."

Lew is equally successful when he interprets Helen's threat to go to the union as an expression of her fear, and asks that she show up for their next meeting.

By imagining out loud, Lew attempts to maintain contact with Helen. Another way he attempts to maintain contact is, paradoxically, by remaining silent at key moments. This skill is first demonstrated in their initial meeting:

"It's all so long ago; this is silly to rehash . . ." Helen's voice began in a tone of rebuff and then trailed off.

I did not speak. It seemed to me that as she began to write off my remarks, some other thought or feeling had intruded itself into her consciousness, thus accounting for the trailing-off quality in her voice. I was curious to see if she would choose to speak that new thought.

Again, a few minutes later, Lew is purposely silent to give Helen a chance to articulate her reactions. Helen accuses him of writing her off in their previous interactions and Lew responds:

"Indeed I did," I said. Helen seemed surprised, a bit discombobulated, actually. I waited a moment to give her a chance to speak, but she didn't.

At still another time, Lew is silent. Helen has just finished saying, "There are parents out there right now, if they knew how you are talking to me . . ." Lew says "How's that?" with real curiosity, "What am I saying to you?"

Helen was caught off guard in that way I'd learned to recognize. Here again, I'd been able not to take her literally and get trapped into automatic counterattack. I was able to realize that I did not know what meanings she had made of these discussions and the information I'd revealed, and I was able to act assertively from my "not knowing" as a resource for inquiry rather than a liability to hide.

There was a long silence.

At other times in the case, Lew is silent because he is confused or does not know what will happen next. That sort of silence is different from the purposeful silence he displays here and repeatedly through the meetings, a silence which appears to be designed to invite further participation and exploration by Helen.

Structuring Interactions

A third set of skills is also used by Lew in his interaction with Helen. These are not skills to which he gives a name. We would call them "structuring." By that term we mean that Lew uses the legitimate authority of his position as a leader to structure situations with Helen. The structuring both sets limits on the interaction and contributes to shifting the quality of the exchange from unilateral to mutual and from competition to learning. It is important because it both does what the consultant did for the learner in setting the stage for learning and it simultaneously acknowledges that the person being addressed did not volunteer.

In this sense, the leader who is modelling his effort on his own learning experience has a more difficult task than the consultant with whom he has worked. The leader is dealing not with someone who chose to come to him to learn but with someone to whom he went and suggested the importance of learning.

In the first meeting with Helen, Lew structures the interaction by initially addressing two aspects of their past history. When she tries to speak, he firmly sets limits by asking her to wait until he has finished, so that she can receive the information in its entirety.

By refusing to allow Helen to dominate him, Lew avoids the consequence of later resenting her for it. In this way Lew minimizes some of the potential for what could emerge as competitive, unilateral behavior on his own part. He sets limits and thereby creates the expectation for a quality of interaction he is hoping will take place.

Lew alters the structure when he responds to Helen's request in the third meeting that they stop early, but he sets forth his expectation for future meetings. This is another of the ways in which he attempts to make their interaction mutual.

During the fourth meeting, Lew structures the interaction by turning Helen's attack on his disciplining of pupils into an invitation to Helen to look at the similarity between their two situations. When she reluctantly recognizes the similarity and opens herself to inquiry, he is able to structure a concrete exercise around her response to Henry.

When, after the fourth meeting, Helen writes a note saying she has made a decision to move to the fifth grade and sees no further need to meet, Lew defends the meetings he has structured and responds with a note saying they do need to meet. When she confronts him in the hall, restating her point about not meeting, and threatening him with a grievance to the union, he again stands behind his hope that they can work together, suggesting that she may be afraid.

The payoff for Lew in his attempts to create a structure which invites learning rather than competition comes in the fifth meeting. After an initial attack, Helen tentatively acknowledges that, "No one's taken the time with me before. . . ." This acknowledgment, in turn, moves directly into her statement that she has thought a lot about their earlier discussions and has already begun to change.

At that point Lew and Helen together structure a series of monthly meetings to prepare for Helen's move to fifth grade. Now the structuring has become more mutual.

While Lew's structuring of the interaction creates the setting in which mutual exploration can take place, the early stages of arranging those meetings are not mutual. Other than adjusting the length of the third meeting to accommodate Helen, Lew dictates the time, place, frequency, and to a large extent, the content of the meetings. Helen shows some willingness to cooperate by coming to the meetings and by not going to the union. However, the paradox remains that initially in order to achieve mutuality, Lew appears dictatorial.

Yet in setting up the meetings, Lew does not attempt to win in the old sense of having the right answer, of giving Helen the negative information and departing, or of firing or replacing her. Instead he commits himself to creating a mechanism for defining the question and developing answers. The structure he creates is designed to give her the information, share his own thinking, accompany her in her attempts to make sense of her responses, get and use new information about his own performance, and mutually create a plan of action. While he is tough-minded in his adherence to the structure he has created, his stance can be viewed as a commitment to the possibility of mutuality, a mutuality which is solidified in the fifth meeting.

Conclusion

Utilizing a number of skills, we have seen Lew seek to engage with Helen in ways that create the conditions for learning for them both. What we witness in Lew appears to be a repertoire of actions from which he can draw where appropriate.

The concept of a repertoire of actions is built on some of the following assumptions:

That there is no best action in a given situation

That it is possible to develop a constellation of different responses which could be appropriate

That it is not necessary to choose between alternatives in advance

That the capacity to have alternatives available in the moment, combined with a commitment to get information from the setting, will determine the appropriateness of the response

Part 5 | CONCLUSION

14 | Redefining Leadership Style

Lew's experience in the previous case can be taken as a summation and extension of the experiences of the other leaders in this book. Because his early definition of leadership is similar to the definitions of Tom, Paul, Steve, and Joe and because his learning is similar also, we tend to think of Lew as an embodiment of their experience as we use him to talk about a redefinition of leadership style.

A number of times through his case, particularly at the beginning and at the end, Lew talks about his old assumptions about effective leadership based on the need to be liked, right, in control, invulnerable, and rational. His new assumptions are clearly not the simple opposite of his old ones. In no way do his actions in the case suggest that instead of being liked, he prefers being disliked; rather than right, wrong; instead of in control, out of control or that he is now vulnerable and irrational rather than invulnerable and rational. Rather what we observe in Lew is an expansion of his assumptions of what it is to be human and to be a leader. These new assumptions do not eliminate the old; the new assumptions render the old assumptions less dominant.

Instead of assuming that to be a good leader he must be liked by others, we see Lew at the end needing to like himself, as he suggests when he says only he can now answer the question, "Did I do the right thing?" He is able most of the time throughout the case to believe in what he is doing, despite

Helen's resistance and attacks, and to honor Helen's resistance as an expression of her integrity.

Instead of assuming that to be a good leader, he must be right, Lew appears to need to learn. He resists a number of opportunities to move in on Helen, assert his view, and -"win." Rather than having his integrity invested in being right and trying to convince Helen and others of his definition of the problem and his solution, Lew seems to have invested his integrity in inquiring and in trying to create a mechanism for defining the questions and arriving at mutual answers.

Instead of assuming that he must take responsibility for controlling information, and thereby controlling Helen, Lew takes responsibility for giving Helen information of a variety of kinds and for inviting a mutual exploration of that information.

Instead of assuming that he must be invulnerable, in the sense of above the action, outside it, protected from it, and seeking to protect others, Lew moves into the situation, confronts Helen, acknowledges his past and present responsibility for that part which he contributed, experiences intense feelings of vulnerability, and also recognizes and honors the way in which exposure and vulnerability evoke a similar response from Helen. In turn, their shared vulnerabilities allow for a quality of interchange that produces a better decision than would have otherwise been the case.

Instead of assuming that he must be rational in the sense of declaring emotions as "off limits" or as illegitimate ways of making sense, Lew simultaneously welcomes a broad range of feelings and becomes more rational in the sense of extraordinarily conscious of, and skilled in responding to, the nuances of feeling and thought within himself and between him and Helen.

What appears to have happened, then, to Lew's old assumptions about self is not that they are no longer relevant or are eliminated by new opposing assumptions, but that they have been subsumed under more embracing assumptions. These new assumptions about himself have been learned, often painfully, and they now give rise in Lew to other related and more general assumptions about human beings. These new assumptions about other people include:

People are basically ambivalent: they want simultaneously to change and to stay the same.

People create their own meanings.

People's resistance can be viewed as an expression of their integrity, not as a case of their being "dumb" or "bad" or "weak."

Caring can be expressed through confrontation not just protection.

Conflict can be productive.

The definition of information can be expanded.

New kinds of information can be appropriately shared.

Mutual dialogue in which new information (often negative) is shared can lead people to make real choices.

An outcome of real choice is a new level of commitment and hope.

These statements sound like the kind of general propositions many people espouse. In Lew's case, they are different because they represent one of the central outcomes of his personal learning. These propositions are consciously chosen assumptions which Lew is capable of putting into deliberate action. These statements therefore represent a fusion of what Lew practices and what Lew preaches.

Another way of saying this is to look at the shifts that occurred in Lew's old personal assumptions about leadership when juxtaposed with his new assumptions about other people. When Lew comes to assume and to be able to act from the assumption that people are ambivalent and that their resistance is an expression of their integrity, not necessarily an expression of their dislike, what happens to his need to be liked? It changes into an appreciation of the separateness of people and the importance of honoring that separateness in himself and in others.

When Lew comes to assume and to act from the assumption that people make their own meaning and that truth is relative, what happens to his need to be right? It becomes invested more in the process of inquiry than in the product of "right" solutions.

When Lew comes to assume and to act from the assumption that mutual commitment produces a higher quality of decision making and yet that people are inherently ambivalent, what happens to his need to take responsibility for controlling information and people? It expands into taking responsibility not for controlling the thoughts and feelings of others but for making clear to himself and to others his own thoughts and feelings.

When Lew comes to assume and to be able to act from the assumption that people can change (because he can change) and that caring can be expressed in confrontation rather than protection, what happens to his need to be invulnerable, separate, outside, above the interaction? It expands into sharing parts of himself (painful as that is) in the hopes of thereby learning more about himself and encouraging others to do the same.

When Lew comes to assume that people are ambivalent and make sense not only through their ideas but through their feelings and the meanings they attach to feelings, what happens to his wish to be rational and to rule off-limits those sense-making processes? Being rational deepens into trying to understand some of the complexity of feeling, thought, and action in himself and ultimately in others.

These appear to be some of the new assumptions Lew is able to act from. Examined in conjunction with his old assumptions, they can be framed as a contrasting set of old and new criteria for judging his effectiveness as a leader:

OLD CRITERIA	REDEFINITION OF	EMERGING CRITERIA
Be liked	Conflict/resistance	Accept one's separateness and honor that of others.
Be right	Knowledge	Inquire through interaction, search for questions and answers.
Be in control	Responsibility	Take responsibility for self but not for thoughts and feelings of others, or for forces over which one can have no control.
Be invulnerable	Caring	Confront as an expression of caring.
Be rational	Information	Maximize amount and kind of information that is shared.

Final Word

While this book may provide techniques for improved interaction, the central point is that the learning which enables the effective use of these techniques is deep-seated. Most fundamentally, the leaders' learning results not just in new techniques but in new ways of interpreting personal and interpersonal events. The trust that comes with the capacity to make new sense and to invent appropriate new actions enables leaders to behave not just more skillfully but more intelligently and courageously.

Another central theme is captured by Kiyo Morimoto's statement, "The shortest way through psychic pain is through the middle." That which terrifies or disgusts us about ourselves, that from which we long to free ourselves—those ambivalences, inner conflicts, feelings we think we should not have, those vulnerabilities, in short—are what we have to face and welcome into full participation in ourselves. We must do this not with the intent of welcoming them in order to be rid of them but of welcoming them with the intent of accepting them as expressions of who we are. When we do that, we are in a position to construct a new way of offering leadership, indeed a new way of being ourselves. Denied, debased, exorcized, those vulnerabilities leave us little foundation on which to build a new definition of leadership or selfhood. Acknowledged, accepted, welcomed, those same vulnerabilities provide the basis for new self-respect and courage.

Appendix:

Materials and Methodology

By BARRY JENTZ

The case stories in this book and the work and ideas which they express did not, as one advance reader said, "fall like virgin snow from the author's head in 1973." Indeed. The case-story form did not suddenly emerge in 1973 with the start of LLC.

I have been interested in and working with variations of the case-story form for fifteen years. In 1964, while teaching technical high school students who would not write more than several scrambled sentences, I experimented with ways of getting the students to tell stories about how they "destroyed" new teachers, like me. Over a period of a year, the stories which gradually emerged were good enough for the school literary magazine editors to publish.

In 1968, working with a group of sixty high school students who were tutoring elementary children, I required the writing of case stories similar to those in this book. From the fall of 1969 until the spring of 1973, I wrote an unpublished book-length case story which focused on my own learning and the learning of eight students over a period of two years at the Murray Road School, the first and longest-running public alternative school in the country.

In each of these situations, as in my work with administrators and other clients, the case-story writing was a vehicle for focusing dialogue between myself and a student about the nature of relationships between people and the nature of the internal relationships—that is, between a person's behavior, the thoughts and feelings which influence behavior, and the assumptions about self and others which underlie and guide behavior. For me, the case story has been a practical methodology for inviting people to become acquainted with the consequences of their actions, with the hopes and assumptions which undergird their actions, and with the possibility of trying out new sequences of assumption, action, and consequence.

Some readers will be curious about the source of the data for the case stories in this book and how the case stories were constructed. Though my methods for collecting data were rigorously thought through and carried out, I do *not* present these cases as research in any strict sense.

From the outset of the LLC Program in 1973, I experimented with a variety of ways to interact with administrators through the written as well as the spoken word. Over a period of four years, these written documents accumulated into large case files on particular administrators. For the most part, these files were built through the following kinds of activities.

My colleagues and I began the LLC Program by interviewing sixty-seven administrators twice on separate occasions for one and one-half hours. The first interview focused on learning, the second on leadership. The questions for the learning interview were:

How did you prepare for this job?

What was useful?

What have you learned on the job?

How have you learned?

The single question for the leadership interview was:

How do you see yourself offering leadership in your particular situation?

These interviews were taped and transcribed or recorded in lengthy field notes. The questions from the two interviews were combined and asked of many of these same administrators in each of two succeeding fall terms in 1974 and 1975. We used a similar procedure for recording the data.

We built the case files in several other ways. I audiotaped much of my consulting work, had the tapes transcribed, and returned the tapes and transcriptions to administrators by prior agreement. Then we used the tapes and transcriptions to further our mutual inquiry into administrative practice. A variation on this methodology was the personal letter. I wrote letters to administrators after our meetings describing my understanding of their thinking about their practice and offering my different perspectives. These letters then became a starting point for further dialogue and additional documentation for the case files.

Finally, in 1976, three years into our program, I selected fifteen administrators in two different groups for a "research" project. Eight of the fifteen had been involved with the LLC Program for one year and participated in every other week one-to-one consultation meetings with me. The other seven administrators had been with the LLC Program since its inception, for three years, and they had worked extensively with me in a variety of learning activities.

Each person agreed in advance to participate in a set of interviews conducted by our LLC documentarian, Nancy Zimmerman. In each meeting with a separate administrator, I participated as an interviewee with the administrator. Nancy asked us to address the following questions and focused on clarifying where we confirmed or disconfirmed one another's perceptions:

How do the two of you see the development of the relationship between you?

How has the relationship affected/not affected your learning?

What have you learned?

How have you learned, other than through this relationship?

How have you translated "learning" into new administrative practice? (Here, the administrator was asked to give concrete, before-and-after snapshots or motion-picture descriptions of the actual behavior and thought they used then and now.)

The interviews were all taped and transcribed. Either the transcription or an edited version was sent to the administrator and, in several instances, led to another interview. One of the two groups chose to share their interview transcripts and met as a group to discuss them.

Of the fifteen participants in this activity, I chose five for this book solely on the basis of richness of concrete data about before-and-after interactions in the work setting and sophistication of thinking about the internal shifts which accounted for the before-and-after differences in behavior.

Unfortunately, the best data I had was from men. Only three of the initial group of fifteen were women, and of those I had extensive contact with only one. As a result, there are no women administrators presented in these case stories. This seems to my colleagues and me a serious and unfortunate limitation to this book.

Using these sources of data in the case files, as well as additional data collected during on-going consultation sessions, I constructed the cases in a before-and-after form representing the way the administrators and I worked together: we often began from a particular interpersonal difficulty they had with a teacher, and, within this context, engaged in the kind of learning they describe in their stories, the result of which was often changed behavior with the teacher. When I finished a case story, I sent it to the administrator whose data I had used and asked him to read it with an eye to veracity, readability, and usefulness. Several administrators had only editorial comments. Two men were able to recall more concrete detail about interaction, so I met with them again; we teased out more detail about their interactions with a teacher, and I rewrote the case story to include that detail.

Although all the men enjoyed their stories, three of them were so taken with their case stories that they shared them with their wives. Their decisions to do so were not taken lightly and must be viewed in light of an ethic which places value on keeping work life separated from home life. The husband-wife discussions which resulted from reading the case stories, though unsettling in some ways and sometimes painful, seem to have strengthened marital relationships and this strength in turn seems to have enhanced job performance.

About the Authors

BARRY C. JENTZ holds his B.A. from Kenyon College and an M.A.T. from the Harvard Graduate School of Education. He has been a consultant to administrators, managers, and teachers in a variety of organizations, mainly educational, since 1969. In 1973 he joined with three other people in starting the Leadership and Learning Cooperative: An In-Service Program for School Leaders. LLC provided the framework for consulting work and for a study of the nature of learning.

JOAN W. WOFFORD holds her B.A. from Bryn Mawr College and her M.A.T. from Yale University. She has been a high school teacher and she has taught graduate courses on educational administration and organizational theory. Since 1967 Ms. Wofford has been involved in research and consultation, first with the Organization for Social and Technical Innovation, in Cambridge, and then as a Partner in Leadership and Learning, Inc., in Lincoln, Massachusetts.